GILL'S IRISH LIVES

G000109696

BERNARD SHAW

JOHN O'DONOVAN

GILL AND MACMILLAN

First published 1983 by
Gill and Macmillan Ltd
Goldenbridge
Dublin 8
with associated companies in
London, New York, Delhi, Hong Kong,
Johannesburg, Lagos, Melbourne,
Singapore, Tokyo

0 7171 1039 7 (paperback)
0 7171 1072 9 (hardback)

available in this series:
Michael Collins (Leon Ó Broin)
Seán O'Casey (Hugh Hunt)
C. S. Parnell (Paul Bew)
James Craig (Patrick Buckland)
James Joyce (Peter Costello)
Eamon de Valera (T. Ryle Dwyer)
Daniel O'Connell (Fergus O'Ferrall)
Theobald Wolfe Tone (Henry Boylan)
Edward Carson (A. T. Q. Stewart)
James Connolly (Ruth Dudley Edwards)
Arthur Griffith (Calton Younger)
Jonathan Swift (Bernard Tucker)
George Bernard Shaw (John O'Donovan)
Oscar Wilde (Richard Pine)
Seán Lemass (Brian Farrell)
W. B. Yeats (Augustine Martin)

Origination by Galaxy Reproductions Ltd, Dublin
Printed in Hong Kong

Contents

Judas: Thou art no common man, why dost thou rot
In this forgotten corner.

Jesus: Be it curst.
I sometimes wish, by Heaven, I had the power
To extinguish it like Sodom — leave not one
Of all who knew my wretched history
Alive to blight me with contemptuous memories.

(from *Passion Play*, an unfinished piece
written by Shaw when he was twenty-two.)

1
The Background

George Bernard Shaw, by birth a Dubliner, detested his native city and his native city did not much care for him either. He told Ellen Terry that he'd had a devil of a childhood there, although there is no evidence that it was the truly fearsome kind of childhood that Samuel Butler and many another man of genius (and of no genius) suffered. His father and mother were, he conceded, quite uncoercive, although his father's allegedly heavy drinking, which his mother bitterly resented, must have created tensions in the household that told heavily on the sensitive boy.

There were other reasons for his dislike of Dublin. The city made him feel inadequate. Regarding himself, as he had been taught, as belonging to a distinguished family of the Anglo-Irish Protestant ascendancy, by definition the natural superiors of the ordinary Irish Catholic majority, he found his daily life bedevilled by contradictions arising from this social distinction. Technically his father was a gentleman, entitled to be addressed as Esquire in correspondence, because although he was in trade it was as a wholesaler. A retailer was an altogether inferior being, merely 'mistered' on envelopes. Yet young Shaw could not help noticing that his father's tailor, Mister Samuel M'Comas, had his Naval, Military & Merchant Tailoring

establishment in the city's main street, while the
[2] Esquire's much shabbier establishment was tucked
away in a side street off the quays of the fearsomely
stinking River Liffey.

Moreover, the tailor, although loftily patronised
by the Esquire, lived in some splendour in Cliff
Castle at Dalkey and had his yacht in Dublin Bay,
while the Esquire and his family shared, with a singing teacher, a small cottage on nearby Torca Hill
for a summer retreat, and could not afford so much
as a canoe.

Catholics, as young Shaw was informed by his
elders, were ignorant, superstitious, fearful of liberty
and therefore not to be entrusted with it. Their
proper employment was as hewers of wood and
drawers of water. Yet many in the amateur musical
society with which his mother was involved were
Catholics and didn't in the least correspond with
this description. Besides, as Shaw was to remark later
on, God had unaccountably vouchsafed much better
voices to the Catholics than to the Protestants. The
society's leading tenor, Charles Cummins, was a
Catholic with a particular devotion to the Virgin
Mary. Yet it was difficult to describe as ignorant
or superstitious this splendid looking tall-hatted
gentleman (he used a sombrero for musical occasions),
who was a prosperous accountant with spacious
offices in the most select part of commercial Dublin
and with another office in the City — the real city:
London.

In the Shaws' neighbourhood were other children
who, although eligible playmates, were prohibited
company to young Shaw because they were Catholic,
Shaw being prohibited to them because he was
Protestant. Those boys were not less well dressed
than he, nor the girls than his sisters, nor were they
less well spoken or, for children, less well mannered.

Their fathers set off like his own father each weekday morning to their offices. Some of them were civil servants in Dublin Castle, and in a great many respects these gentlemen weren't really much different from his own father.

Of course not many of these fathers were in the Esquire's happy position of having a baronet for a second cousin. But on the other hand their houses were more spacious and looked more comfortable than No. 3 Upper Synge Street (later renumbered 33 Synge Street) where George Bernard Shaw, youngest child and only son, had been born on 26 July 1856. Moreover, higher standards of house-keeping were maintained in most of those other houses than in No. 3, where Mrs Shaw had abandoned her three children to a nurse (of whom Shaw had fond recollections), and the housekeeping to an £8-a-year maid of all work, the better to be able to devote herself wholly to the work of the amateur musical society. She made orchestral arrangements of piano scores, copied band parts, and was generally the chief lieutenant and right hand of the society's energetic director and conductor, George John Lee.

Lee lived around the corner in Harrington Street in a larger and more fashionable house than the Shaws'. But he was so much in and out of No. 3, and so much at home there, that he seemed to young Shaw to be a kind of supplementary father and husband.

Then there was Walter John Gurly, ship's surgeon and Mrs Shaw's brother, who stayed with them while on shore leave (God knows where they rigged up a bed for him), and he too was so much at home there that he made a third father. If, said Shaw later on, he'd had three mothers as well as three fathers, he'd have backed himself against any man in the world. And when, later on, the contradictions which puzzled his childhood had been resolved in the light of [4] maturity, Shaw discovered another reason for not liking his native city. He had become aware that his character both as man and as author had been flawed by human failings which Dublin, more than other cities, seems to develop inordinately in its sons and daughters: chiefly a nastily begrudging attitude to almost everyone else, and an even nastier grinning derision about activities and aspirations which civilised communities regard as praiseworthy. As a non-smoking teetotal vegetarian he would have been classed as a bit of a crank in any community, but Dublin felt that refusal to take part in an evening's drinking was a hostile act, or at least insufferably standoffish. Shaw's offence was compounded by an icy distaste for smutty stories, particularly the kind of smut which was utterly without point or humour, although this was the staple of conversation for many of his contemporaries.

Perhaps it is not fair to single out Dublin for an indictment which could be brought against Ireland as a whole. After all it was not merely Dubliners but the Irish in general who were the subject of Dr Johnson's too-oft quoted observation. But Shaw's Irish experience was mainly a Dublin experience, for in his youth he hardly knew any other part of Ireland apart from what he learned of the depressing little town of Newry, some sixty miles away to the North, which he visited when his friend Mathew Edward McNulty was posted to the Bank of Ireland branch there. His dislike of Ireland and the Irish was accordingly concentrated on Dublin.

2

Shaw wasn't far off the mark in reporting that his family's pride was so enormous that they habitually spoke of themselves as the Shaws, as who should say the Hohenzollerns or the Habsburgs. The founder of [5] the Irish Shaws was William Shaw, who came over from Hampshire as a captain in King William III's army, fought at the Boyne and was duly rewarded with handsome grants of forfeited land in counties Kilkenny and Cork. In the following generations the Shaws went into the professions, one branch settling in Co. Cork. In the 1770s Robert Shaw, a great-grandson of Captain William, set up as a merchant in Dublin, in Capel Street, prospered and became Comptroller of Sorting at the Post Office, in 1784. The following year he leased a gentleman's residence, Terenure House, which had thirty-five acres of pleasure grounds. An adjoining property, Bushy Park, was acquired a few years later, apparently as an investment, by Abraham Wilkinson, a rich silk merchant with an only child, Maria. Wilkinson himself lived not far away in Mount Jerome.

In January 1796 Robert Shaw's eldest son, another Robert, married Maria Wilkinson, getting with her Bushy Park and £10,000. The following July Robert senior died, aged forty-seven. Young Robert, aged twenty-two, was now rich enough to cut a dash around town. But he didn't. In 1799 he bought a partnership in a bank recently founded by Thomas Lighton, an ordinary soldier who had returned from service in India with a romantically acquired fortune. In 1805 Lighton died and was replaced as partner by Ponsonby Shaw, a younger brother of Robert. The bank, from now on known as Shaw's Bank, operated until 1836 when the partners sold out to the newly formed Royal Bank of Ireland.

Robert took an energetic part in public life. He sat for Dublin in the Westminster parliament, having previously sat for Bannow, Co. Wexford, (not New Ross as stated in the Peerage) in the College Green parliament, was a colonel of militia, a member of the Royal Irish Academy, and was on the committee, of which Arthur Guinness was another member, which organised the erection of Nelson Pillar in Dublin's main thoroughfare. Robert was also Lord Mayor of the city (1815-16), and was created a baronet in August 1821 during George IV's visit to Ireland.

Amongst the baronet's grand-uncles was one Bernard (a name which had become popular in the family). Bernard, of Kilkenny, was an attorney and notary public, who is said to have been swindled out of a large sum of money, dying in consequence of a broken heart at the age of fifty-three in 1826. This Bernard had married Frances Carr, daughter of a Co. Waterford rector. She was one of the women who brought longevity into the Shaw family, surviving until 1871 when she died at the age of eighty-eight years and eight months after a widowhood of forty-five years.

Among her many children (reputedly fourteen) was George Carr Shaw, born on 30 December 1814, the Esquire of the previous pages, and second cousin of the banker baronet. Two of the Esquire's brothers emigrated to Australia whence, a century later, there arrived in Europe a cousin of GBS's, Charles MacMahon Shaw, with the manuscript of a highly romantic family history entitled *Bernard's Brethren* which was published in 1939 with tart annotations by Bernard.

The Esquire's eldest brother married into the landed gentry (Putland of Bray Head and of Sarsfield's Court, Co. Cork), but the couple separated and William Bernard Shaw ended in a mental home, succumbing to a heart attack brought on (according to GBS) by an attempt to decapitate himself by snapping a portmanteau shut on his neck.

The youngest of the brothers, Richard Frederick, became chief clerk at the Valuation Office, an [7] influential enough position to make a well-known land agent willing to provide a berth in his office for the young George Bernard.

A sister, Cecilia, married her first cousin Rev. William George Carroll, rector of St Bride's in Dublin. Their fathers had married daughters of Rector Carr, and Carroll came from Bannow, which had been represented in the old College Green parliament by Robert Shaw. Rev. Carroll performed the marriage ceremony for the Esquire and in due course baptised the children and taught Latin to the boy.

We know nothing of the Esquire's upbringing and education except that he was often hungry as a child and therefore insisted that plenty of bread and butter should always be within reach of his own children. He was only twelve when his father died, and was probably more neglected at this important period of his life than would have been the case with the eldest and youngest of the family. He may even have been bullied more than a little by his elder brothers, for GBS was to comment upon his timidity and for-bearance. The way he was bossed by his wife and elbowed aside in his own house by the intrusive singing teacher and by the ship's surgeon, suggest that he had less than average self-assertiveness.

Early in her widowhood his mother had been given a cottage in Terenure (then called Roundtown) by the banker baronet, her cousin-in-law. Here she lived with her eleven surviving children until most of them were dispersed through marriage or emigration. Either with hope or with humour she called the cottage Harmony Cottage, although the allusion may have been purely musical, for according to GBS all the Shaws seemed able to play any brass instrument at sight. Such must have been the crush in Harmony

Cottage that the Esquire, when himself a householder,
[8] may not have noticed any overcrowding in No. 3
Upper Synge Street, even when Lee's choir and
orchestra were rehearsing in the front room.

3

According to the 1851 census, Dublin city had
258,361 people living in 24,317 houses, an average
of something over ten to a house. The Liffey halved
the city into Northside and Southside, and the
Dubliners of those days gave the impression of
knowing everyone else in their own half, with quite
a few knowing everyone else in the other half as well.
The following sketch of the Esquire's business career
— we shall refer to him as George Carr Shaw or GCS
from now on — demonstrates how closely interwoven
were the lives of those Dubliners.

In his twenties GCS worked in the Phoenix Iron-
works in Parkgate Street. It was then owned by
William Robinson, one of four brothers with fine
voices who were prominent in Dublin music during
most of the nineteenth century. One brother, Joseph,
an indefatigable organiser of concerts and the man
who introduced Dublin to Beethoven's Ninth
Symphony (appropriately enough in the year Shaw
was born), was the chief founder of what became the
Royal Irish Academy of Music. He was also a friend
and encourager of Lee, who was presently to irrupt
into GCS's little household. This raises the interesting
possibility that GCS knew Lee, or knew of him, even
before his wife did.

In 1838 or thereabouts GCS went to work in the
office of Todhunters, Rogerson's Quay, one of those
astonishingly versatile Dublin firms which dealt more
or less under the same roof in grotesquely unrelated
commodities. Todhunters specialised in slates and

tiles, corn and flour. The son of the family, John, became a doctor and exercised the family talent for versatility by publishing an algebra and practising as an untalented amateur playwright. When his progenitors departed for the next world, leaving him well provided for, Dr Todhunter departed for London around about the same time as Shaw did. The Todhunter-Shaw acquaintance continued in London for several years, and was presently enlarged to include Yeats *père et fils*. It was Todhunter's dismally failing *Comedy of Sighs* which was replaced by Shaw's sparkling *Arms and the Man* in the short Shaw-Todhunter-Yeats season mounted at the Avenue Theatre in London in 1892.

After about seven years in the Todhunter office, George Carr Shaw left to take up a minor post in the Four Courts which had in all probability been secured for him through the influence of his cousin Frederick Shaw, Recorder of Dublin and a younger son of the banker baronet. Six years later, this post having been abolished, GCS retired on a pension of £44 a year, shortly afterwards joining Haughtons, corn factors, whose main business was in Carlow. After about six months he moved to yet another corn factors, Wilsons, from whom he went to work for still another factors, MacMullen, Shaw & Co. of Burgh Quay. The Shaw was his younger brother Henry who, on becoming a widower, married MacMullen's daughter (1861). The company also included Joseph Henry O'Brien, who was also running a flour business of his own in South King Street.

O'Brien bought GCS's Four Courts pension for £500 (insuring the pensioner's life for £600). With this money GCS bought a partnership in the milling firm run by George Clibborn, who had previously been in partnership with Henry Shaw. (Thus the partnership Clibborn & Shaw had two phases, each

with a different Shaw.) We need not deduce from
GCS's turnover of employments that he was the
ne'er-do-well of the family, although it does give us
grounds for suspecting that drink began to be a
problem with him while he was still a young man.
The author of *Bernard's Brethren* maintains that GCS
was not a dipsomaniac and that Shaw, being a teetotaller, may have unwittingly exaggerated the
extent of his father's drinking. 'One glass of beer',
says MacMahon Shaw, 'is enough to turn a man into
a drunkard when teetotallers smell his breath.'
(p. 123) But there exists a notebook in which Shaw
entered odds and ends of family history and such
like (*c.* 1870s) in which he describes the drinking
habits of an unidentified person he was intimately
acquainted with, a person who sounds remarkably
like his father. This description and the note about
his father in *Bernard's Brethren* accord closely,
leaving one with little doubt that GCS was for many
years an alcoholic.

Shaw's mother's people, the Carlow Gurlys, were
not the landed gentry he and his sister Lucy liked to
believe they were, their recorded possession of
sixteen acres of land (valuation, £15. 15s. 0d.) hardly
putting them in this class. Ryan's *History of Carlow*
doesn't include them in its catalogue of locally
notable families. They were mostly attorneys and
army men, and one member of the family was a
chancellor of the diocese. There is a monument to
an eighteenth-century Gurly in Carlow parish church,
and there used to be a laneway in the town called
Gurly Lane. The Gurly property Shaw inherited from
his uncle and eventually municipalised, consisted
of buildings in the town, none of great importance.

The Gurlys may have been connected in some way
with a family of true landed gentry, the Bagenals of
Bennerkerry, who owned 1,309 acres of Co. Carlow

land. Shaw's maternal grandfather was named Walter Bagenal (sometimes spelt Bagnel, sometimes Bagnall) after one of them. The Gurlys' chief hope of financial salvation lay in peddling their pretensions to gentility amongst the moneyed but un-blueblooded. Into this category came the Whitcrofts. John Whitcroft, believed by Shaw to have been the illegitimate son of a Somebody, made enough money out of pawnshops in the Rev. Carroll's parish of St Bride's to establish himself in a small country house at Whitechurch in the Dublin foothills (his neighbour being a banker colleague of Sir Robert Shaw), and to make his eldest son a barrister. The son in turn became owner of 2,267 acres in Co. Kilkenny, with undisputed status as a squire.

Whitcroft's daughter Lucinda was still unmarried at twenty-seven, a rather late age for those times. Somewhere, somehow she had met Walter Bagenal Gurly, described by Shaw as a wiry, tight, smallish hardknit man with a toughened face and short ginger whiskers in the Franz Josef style. Shaw adds that Gurly was very handy, able to do anything except manage his affairs and 'keep his estate from slipping through his fingers' (letter to Frank Harris, 5 June 1930). *What* estate? one might ask. Shaw gives another significant fact about his grandfather. He was able to ride horses, bought by their owners for £200 but so unmanageable as to have to be sold for £20. This strongly suggests that Gurly's income, like Flurry Knox's in the Somerville and Ross stories, came from horse dealing. One wonders whether the acquaintance between Gurly and the Whitcrofts mightn't have been established against a background of clattering hooves.

Gurly and Lucinda Whitcroft were married in Dublin in 1829. Lucinda gave birth the following year to Lucinda Elizabeth, future mother of GBS.

After ten years of marriage, which in Gurly's financial circumstances can hardly have been ideally happy, Mrs Gurly died, leaving, besides her nine-year-old daughter, a son of about four. This was Shaw's future Rabelaisian uncle, Walter John Gurly, the ship's surgeon.

The orphaned girl was now entrusted to the care of an aunt, her mother's youngest sister, the hump-backed sweet-faced Ellen Whitcroft of the Shaw saga, whom Shaw always referred to as rich. The general understanding was that she would make Lucinda Elizabeth her heiress. But Ellen wasn't all that rich, for when she died in 1862 at the age of fifty, she proved to have been worth only 'under £4,000'. Even on the financial scale of those days this was hardly great wealth.

Ellen may have taken charge of her orphaned nephew too, although he later appears to have been taken over by the Kilkenny squire. Both children were educated more expensively, presumably at the expense of the Whitcrofts, than they could have been by their father. Walter was sent to Kilkenny College, described with some justification by GBS as 'then the Eton of Ireland' (although Portora and St Columba's might not altogether accept this). While he was the smallest boy in the school he used squeeze out under the gate to make assignations on behalf of the senior lads with the Kilkenny whores, maintaining in later life that boarding schools for boys should always be near enough to towns for the pupils to have access to women and thus save themselves from homosexuality. One gets the feeling that Walter John was a chip off the old block.

Lucinda Elizabeth, known in the family as Bessie, would probably have been taught at home by her aunt and/or by a governess. In due course she was sent to learn music from a fashionable Dublin teacher,

Johann Bernhard Logier, a German immigrant who prided himself on an abominable invention called the chiroplast, a contraption for holding a pupil's hands rigidly in position as they travelled up and down the keyboard. Either in spite of or because of the chiroplast, Bessie did not play with any great skill or feeling, if her son is allowed to be the judge. But she had gained one ability from Logier's tuition: the ability to vamp accompaniments and improvise missing orchestral parts thanks to a grounding in her teacher's treatise, *Thoroughbass*, reputed to have been Wagner's first textbook.

Gurly was meanwhile borrowing endlessly from Ellen Whitcroft on the strength of IOUs. It may seem strange that Ellen, characterised by GBS as a determined and forceful little woman who had imposed an extremely rigorous training upon Bessie, should have proved such an easy touch for her brother-in-law. The likely explanation is that Gurly would have held the threat over Ellen Whitcroft of removing his children from her care, thus creating a painful void in the spinster's life. Indeed the word blackmailer is not too strong to apply to Walter Bagenal Gurly in view of what we know of his financial dealings.

There was a decidedly forceful vein in both the Whitcrofts and the Gurlys, of which Bessie inherited an ample share. It seems that in her late teens she rebelled against her aunt's discipline and either went to live with her father or paid lengthy visits to him. There is no record of his ever having been a householder. He moved from place to place, living either as a boarder or as a guest with friends. At this period he was staying in a house called Parson's Green in Kilmacud, near Stillorgan, now a South Dublin suburb but then a small village offering plenty of facilities to the sportsman. He still kept in touch with Carlow friends, with two corn merchants in particular, Samuel Haughton and Simeon Clarke. In [14] the spring of 1852 he 'unexpectedly' — the term is Shaw's — set about marrying Simeon Clarke's daughter, Elizabeth Anne. Clarke was supposed to be heavily indebted to Gurly, who 'perhaps thought it best to cement this financial alliance with a more sentimental one'.

What Shaw did not reveal, perhaps because he did not know, was that Gurly's marriage to Elizabeth Anne on 25 May 1852 in Dublin, instead of in the bride's home town of Carlow, took place two months after the birth of the first of the couple's six daughters.

Their marriage had been held up because news of the impending event was given, perhaps inadvertently, perhaps not, by Bessie to her Uncle John Whitcroft, who promptly had the bridegroom arrested for debt when he issued from his quarters on his wedding morning to buy a pair of gloves. Gurly for his part believed that Bessie had deliberately informed on him to her uncle in order to prevent the marriage. Bessie now had to choose between living with an enraged father and a probably equally enraged stepmother or returning to subordination to the tyrannous Aunt Ellen. At this juncture a third choice presented itself. She could accept the proposal of the thirty-eight-year-old George Carr Shaw.

How she came to be acquainted with GCS we are not told. One possibility is that while living with her father she met the Clarkes and their Carlow colleague Haughton, in whose Dublin office GCS was working. GCS's proposal may have been the outcome of love, pure and undefiled, for the twenty-two-year-old girl. He may never have given a thought to her being the presumed heiress of her aunt and the joint beneficiary with her brother of a trust fund that had been set up by the pawnbroker. But, as the Duke of Wellington remarked in another connection, if you can believe

that you can believe anything. Mingled with what- [15]
ever feeling GCS had for Bessie must have been some
regard for her financial prospects.

She was warned that GCS was a drunkard. She
asked him if this was so. GCS replied that he was a
convinced teetotaller. Shaw, while assuring us that he
would not attempt to defend his father for telling
this lie, then proceeds to defend him by explaining
that GCS was a teetotaller in theory, failing only in
putting theory into practice. Bessie however accepted
GCS's statement *au pied de la lettre* and they were
married in St Peter's, 'the parish church of Dublin,'
on 17 June 1852, the bridgroom's brother-in-law
Rev. Carroll officiating, the witnesses being Gurly
(apparently having forgiven Bessie for the occasion),
and George Henry MacMullen, the corn factor in
whose office GCS had recently, and may still have
been, employed. Seven months previously Jane
Francesca Elgee had married Dr William Wilde in
this church, becoming in 1854 the parents of Oscar.

Just before marriage, GCS was living at No. 17
Lennox Street. For his first matrimonial home he
was to move only a matter of yards around the corner
into Upper Synge Street, then a terrace of quite
newly built houses with open fields opposite. No. 3
was a smallish house, two storeys over basement. On
the hallway storey there was a parlour-cum-diningroom
which looked out onto the street, with a bedroom
behind, and upstairs a relatively large drawingroom,
with the master bedroom at the back. At the end
of the hallway, a small return room; downstairs,
kitchen, maid's room and pantry, with an outdoor
w.c. in the back yard. It was in the upstairs bedroom
that Shaw was born in the early hours of 26 July
1856 to the twenty-six-year-old Bessie. His father was
forty-two. They already had two daughters, Lucinda
Frances, born 26 March 1853, nine months and nine

days after the marriage; and Agnes Elinor, for whose arrival we have no precise date. The girls were known in the family as Lucy and Yuppy, Shaw being Sonny after an initial brief period as Bob.

There may have been another child after Shaw, a miscarriage rather than an actual birth, because in the summer of 1857 Bessie did a most unusual thing. She went off with the four-year-old Lucy on a six-week visit to her father, whose wanderings had then taken him to Kinlough, a village in Co. Leitrim. It wasn't a case of going home to father (in the absence of mother), because there exists a sequence of letters written by GCS from Dublin to his wife, the chatty and affectionate nature of which testify to a good relationship between the two. For a girl like Bessie who lived in cities all her life, a prolonged visit to a remote Irish village is puzzling. Gynaecological trouble arising either from Shaw's birth or from a later pregnancy would plausibly explain one odd feature of Bessie's marriage: that it produced only three children. The Shaws were, as a clan, extremely prolific.

But there may have been another reason for this: the arrival of the cuckoo in the nest, George John Lee.

2
The Cuckoo in the Nest

1

In the Shaw biographies that appeared during their subject's lifetime and for a decade afterwards, there isn't a word about George John Lee (later George Vandeleur Lee), which doesn't derive from Shaw himself. Nor does Lee appear in any reference book I have been able to trace except James D. Brown's one-volume *Biographical Dictionary of Musicians* (1888) which says that he was an 'English writer, author of "The Voice, its Artistic Production, Development, and Preservation," 4to, 1870, 2 editions'. The early editions of *Grove's Dictionary* do not mention Lee. Even more strangely there is nothing about him in the memoirs of Dublin musicians of that period, although there is one reference to him (without naming him) in Vignoles's *Life of Sir Robert P. Stewart* which shall be examined presently.

Shaw said he knew nothing of Lee's background. The statement need not be taken literally because references to Lee which he made at various times show that his ignorance of Lee's origin was not total. One important fact was deliberately suppressed by Shaw. What was Lee's religion? Shaw alleged that he was an agnostic and that music 'was the only religion he ever professed'. This is untrue, and Shaw knew it.

To understand why Shaw lied about Lee's religion in much the same way as his father lied to Bessie

about his teetotallism, we must turn to Shaw's
[18] *Sixteen Self Sketches*, published at the end of his
life, to a chapter of confession entitled 'Shame and
Wounded Snobbery: A Secret Kept for 80 Years'.
The secret was no more than that from February to
September in 1869 the thirteen-year-old Shaw was
a pupil at the Central Model Boys' School in
Marlborough Street in Dublin. The trouble with the
school was that although in theory classless and
undenominational it was in fact lower class and
Roman Catholic, most of the pupils being the sons
of petty shopkeepers and tradesmen. For the son of
a Protestant merchant-gentleman to have to associate
with such boys was a snob tragedy for Shaw akin to
Dickens's enforced employment at the blacking
factory. Shaw says that from the moment he passed
behind the school's unclimbable railings he was
ostracised by other Protestant boys. And Lee was the
cause of his being sent there.

For eighty years, says Shaw, he could not bring
himself to mention the Marlborough Street episode,
not even to his wife. But on making a clean breast
of it, and a clear brain, he was 'completely cured'.
But he wasn't. For he still was unable to confess the
more important part of the secret: that Lee, his
mother's teacher and mentor, close associate and
joint householder, was himself a Roman Catholic.
The case was even blacker. All the leading members
of the Amateur Musical Society were Catholics, and
Bessie had gone so far as to enter Roman Catholic
chapels (as Shaw admitted) to sing Mozart masses
under Lee's direction, and also to take part in fund-
raising concerts for Catholic charities. The point is
vividly illustrated by the well-known group photograph of Lee and his friends. The only two Protestants
in it are Mr and Mrs Shaw. All the others are
Catholics.

Whatever Lee in his Dublin period may have said in private about Catholicism, in public he professed it, remaining on excellent terms with the priests, especially with his namesake (though no relation) Very Rev. Walter Canon Lee, parish priest of Bray. When his mother and brother died, he had them buried in Glasnevin Cemetery, the recognised Catholic necropolis in spite of being, like the Marlborough Street school, in theory undenominational.

Twenty years ago I described in *Shaw and the Charlatan Genius* the researches leading to my discovery of Lee's Catholicism and his background. They need only be summarised here. Shaw tells us that Lee said he never attended a school but was taught by a tutor until in a fit of anger he drove the tutor out of the house with a fishing rod. This is not true. Lee and his younger brother William (later expanded to Harcourt William Nassau) were enrolled in 1838, at the age of eight and seven respectively, in the Christian Brothers School in Dublin's North Richmond Street (popularly known as O'Connell's Schools, Daniel O'Connell having laid the foundation stone in 1828). The names of the parents are stated in the roll to be Robert and Eliza Lee, and their address, Portland Place.

Later on, however, Lee would not allow that Robert was his real father. He claimed more distinguished paternity than the small-time Dublin coal merchant accorded him in the school roll, letting it be known that he was born in Kilrush, Co Clare, the natural son of Colonel Crofton Moore Vandeleur, M.P., J.P., D.L., of Kilrush House; 4 Rutland Square, Dublin; the Kildare Street Club; the Carlton Club, London S.W., and lord of 20,206 acres of counties Clare and Limerick, which alone would have yielded him an income of not less than £16,000 a year in that fortunate era when Prime Minister Gladstone apologised to the nation for having to increase the income tax from 5d. to 6½d. to finance one of the Empire's little wars. The Vandeleurs were of course staunchly Protestant.

No record of the marriage of Robert and Eliza Lee or of the baptism of George or William survives in the Kilrush Catholic or Protestant registers. I use 'survives' deliberately, for on examining the Protestant register I found that four pages recording baptisms and marriages between 1831 and 1833, the vital years of the search, had been carefully removed. The then rector of Kilrush assured me that the registers had not been tampered with in his time (he having become rector in 1945). My guess is that the pages disappeared around 1872, for in December 1871 Lee began to advertise his concerts as under the direction of G. V. Lee, the first time he had used this form of his name in press announcements. At the time of my discovery I believed that the removal of pages from a parish register was a daring and unique act. I have since found from experience that while daring it may have been, unique it certainly was not, either in Ireland or in England. Missing pages are a common feature of such registers.

2

Robert Lee died in January 1843, aged forty-one according to the Glasnevin records. I haven't been able to find where Eliza and her sons lived between 1845 and 1850, but in 1851 she turns up as occupant of No. 2 Portobello Place, a small house about two hundred yards from Shaw's birthplace. Its rateable valuation was £5. 10s. 0d. Not later than 1853 Eliza and her sons moved to No. 16 Harrington Street (later re-numbered 48), the superiority of which as a residence to Portobello Place is reflected in its £34 valuation. The valuation of the Shaw house in nearby [21] Synge Street was £16. One wonders whether Lee, on coming of age, had gained possession of money the Vandeleurs might have settled upon him. In 1853 he is also listed in the directories as occupying part of No. 11 Harrington Street, at that time only three houses away from the Shaw home in Upper Synge Street. In other words, a matter of a few yards separated the dwelling places of Lee and Shaw's mother as early as 1853, three years before Shaw was born. In all his communications to biographers and other enquirers, Shaw never mentioned this. Perhaps he did not know it. If he did it would certainly have added to his perturbed speculations concerning his paternity.

The crucial question is: just when did Bessie first meet Lee? It is out of the question that she wouldn't have quickly got to know so near a neighbour in a friendly and inquisitive little city like Dublin. It wasn't as if Lee wouldn't be noticed in a crowd, if for no other reason than that he had a bad limp, one leg being considerably shorter than the other, the result of a fall downstairs in childhood. (For what it is worth, it can be mentioned here that Shaw himself was much given to falling down stairs and tumbling off rocks, finally toppling off a ladder at the age of ninety-four.)

The record shows that the Amateur Musical Society, of which Lee was the sole lord and master, was founded in 1852; that Bessie was Lee's prima donna and lieutenant in the society, although not necessarily from the start; that Lee trained her voice according to his 'Method,' a four-year process, so that it is within the limits of the possible that George John Lee could have fathered George Bernard Shaw. There are undeniable signs in Shaw's *oeuvre* that he at least considered this possibility himself, for the illegitimacy theme recurs in his plays again and again. Characters who don't know who their father was include Vivie Warren and Frank Gardner in *Mrs Warren's Profession*; the three Clandon children in *You Never Can Tell* (Mrs Clandon with her two daughters and one son has certain striking resemblances to Mrs George Carr Shaw and *her* two daughters and one son); Essie the orphan in *The Devil's Disciple*; Andrew Undershaft and Adolphus Cusins in *Major Barbara*; Julius Baker in *Misalliance*; and in the early novel *Cashel Byron's Profession* Cashel tells the heroine that he knows nothing about his actress mother's people, for she boxed his ears one day 'for asking who my father was'. Most startling of all is a passage in the so-called Frank Harris biography of Shaw, which we now know was virtually written by Shaw:

> All through, from his earliest childhood, he had lived a fictitious life through the exercise of his incessant imagination . . . It was a secret life: its avowal would have made him ridiculous. It had one oddity. The fictitious Shaw was not a man of family. He had no relations. He was not only a bastard, like Dunois or Falconbridge, who at least knew who their parents were: he was also a foundling.

When Shaw was twenty-eight and in London he wrote 'Un Petit Drame' in French, identified in the Bodley Head edition of the plays as an exercise done for Mrs Pakenham Beatty ('Chère Madame') who was giving him lessons in the language. The dialogue incorporates several family references, one character ('Harry') strongly suggesting GCS:

> HARRY (*sobbing*) Abandoned, forsaken, ruined — all gone — wife, children, furniture, everything! . . . Cecily, my daughter, has left me . . . And my friend

Farleigh — he had, I think, treated me most un-
fairly . . .

For Cecily read Lucy, for Farleigh (Far-Lee) the singing teacher, and it looks as if Chère Madame is being
let in on a family joke. Who then is surprised to find
Shaw continually stressing his physical resemblance
to his father? He claimed that one picture of himself
pleased him greatly because it reminded him so much
of his father, which is rather odd because he neither
liked nor admired GCS. His boyhood friend McNulty
records in his so far unpublished Shaw memoir that,
'From an early age George Bernard hated and
despised his weak, inefficient father as much as he
admired his masterful mother.' One does not
normally rejoice in physically resembling a person
one neither likes nor admires. Unless, of course,
there is an ulterior motive.

Shaw assured an early biographer, an Irish-American
named Thomas Demetrius O'Bolger, son of a policeman and author of a historical study of the Battle
of the Boyne, that he hadn't one trait even remotely
resembling any of Lee's. Yet what he said of Lee
could be even more appropriately said of himself:
heterodox and original, mesmeric vitality, active
volcano, fine ear and fastidious taste, always a man
apart. Then we have McNulty attributing to Lee 'a
volubility of language which made him easily one of
the most tireless (if not tiresome) of conversation-
alists,' which pretty well undermines Shaw's claim to
have been totally unlike his mother's hero, and his own.

Shaw gibed at O'Bolger for going around sus-
piciously sniffing at facts like his father the
policeman. But it cannot reasonably be denied that
a biographer has every right, has in fact the policeman's duty, to suspect the suspicious. When Shaw,
having cast Lee in the role of mesmeric genius, was

asked by O'Bolger for some supporting evidence beyond mere assertion, he turned nasty. O'Bolger was told that if it didn't suit his story to believe that Lee was a genius *'in his way'* — and here, you will notice, Shaw has unobtrusively shifted ground — then O'Bolger had better alter his story. 'I tell you that he was and I know better than you, having been an expert music critic who has heard all the great conductors of my time and heard pupils of all the great teachers of singing.' But of all the others who knew Lee and his work, and were qualified to be as good judges as Shaw so far as experience of musicmaking went, not one can be found to share Shaw's enthusiasm. What we do have is one who flatly contradicts him.

Sir Robert Stewart, professor of music at Dublin's Trinity College, and professor of composition at the Royal Irish Academy of Music, official composer to the Viceroy and organist at the city's two Anglican cathedrals, may not himself have been an impressive composer or an inspiring conductor of Nikisch calibre, but he had judgment enough to recognise that the then reviled and ridiculed Wagner was in truth a great genius. Stewart at forty did not come to this conclusion as Shaw did at seventeen. Shaw, then in process of teaching himself the keyboard, had bought a piano score of *Lohengrin*, and half a century later recollected being converted by the first few bars, not, by the way, the most remarkable in that opera. Stewart, without any advantage of hindsight, based his verdict upon performances he had heard in London and in Bayreuth. Stewart was, moreover, a mature and experienced musician with considerable natural endowment. It was jokingly said of him what was near enough to the truth: that he could accompany cathedral evensong with one hand, answer his correspondence with the other, all the while whispering harmony instruction to a pupil.

In a MS note in Stewart's copy of Levey & [25]
O'Rorke's *History of the Theatre Royal, Dublin*,
now in the collection of the Dublin City Library,
Pearse Street he described Lee as 'an arrant imposter,'
and he congratulated himself on driving him out
of Dublin.

Shaw cannot justly be said to have dissented *in
toto* from that opinion. He tells us that after a few
years in London Lee degenerated into a charlatan and
a humbug, this being partly caused by a general
physical degeneration brought about by a slackening
of his Dublin self-discipline. Since Lee died of a heart
attack at fifty-six, that very popular age for so doing,
Shaw's attempt at a scientific explanation of how a
mesmeric and virtuous genius on one side of the Irish
Sea turns into a humbugging charlatan on the other
shouldn't impose on a baby. So far as the truth and
sincerity of his estimate of Lee can now be established, the probability is that in Dublin Shaw, raw
and inexperienced, was dazzled. In London, a
maturer Shaw could view Lee against a metropolitan
background and in the context of performances by
Richter, Manns, and Wagner himself, and reacted by
contemptuously demoting the former hero. It is
amusingly characteristic of Shaw to attribute the
change to a change in Lee and not in the least to any
change in his own experience and standards.

3

That Lee quickly dominated No. 3 Upper Synge
Street is beyond question. He came, he saw, he conquered, although we are unlikely ever to know the
true extent of his conquest. He might have come to
the Shaw house to give Bessie singing lessons much
earlier in her married life than Shaw would have us

believe. (It was the custom in those days for the teacher to come to a lady pupil's home.) The availability nearby of a teacher might have induced her to resume the music lessons she had become used to in her girlhood. She might have seen the development of her musical ability partly as a relief from the tedium of the vacant hours of married life, partly, perhaps, as a reinforcement of her not particularly strong personal attractiveness. A flirtation might have started between her and Lee, a mesmeric young man of her own age, in accordance with the immemorial custom of music masters and their young lady pupils. The flirtation might have developed more alarmingly than she had bargained for. She might even have been caught kissing the teacher. Indeed, an alternative explanation of that puzzling six-weeks' visit to her disliked father and stepmother in the wilds of Co. Leitrim might be that it was an attempt to make her heart less fond through absence. A tolerant and understanding husband, bearing in mind that she is sixteen years younger and giddier than he, writes her affectionate letters, in one of which occurs this passage:

> I delivered your kisses to Yup and Bob but contrary to your instructions I fobbed a few for myself — you know how sweet a stolen kiss is!

The reference to the stolen kiss may be an arch reminiscence of their own courtship or a snide dig at her over Lee. (I believe it is the former.) She returns. The cure, if any, is only temporary. Lee's visits are resumed.

Shaw of course would have none of this. He recalls his first meeting with Lee, when the teacher took him on his lap and embellished him with burnt cork mustachios, a piece of horseplay much resented by the victim. Other vivid recollections include the death of the Prince Consort (December 1861) which caused the newspapers to come out with heavy black lines, and the death of Aunt Ellen (January 1862), the announcement of which by his father obliged him to seek refuge in the tiny back garden to cry his heart out with a sorrow he expected to last his life but in fact lasted only half an hour. It would be reasonable, therefore, to place the Lee recollection in this period, making Shaw about five at the time, thus leaving ample distance between his conception and the arrival of Lee in the household to remove his legitimacy from the shadow of doubt. He did not want his mother, he said, to be the heroine of another Wagner-Geyer lie.

This was an unfortunate parallel to cite in the circumstances. Ernest Newman has proved that Wagner was quite sure he was Geyer's son.

Although the Amateur Musical Society had been founded in 1852 its activities are not recorded for us until 1858, in which year it gave a concert in aid of the Royal Irish Academy of Music which netted £5 for the Academy. Another concert the following year benefitted the Academy to the tune (if you'll pardon the expression) of £25. But the society didn't really get into its stride until the 1860s, its choral and orchestral concert in honour of the Shakespeare Tercentenary in 1864 establishing it as one of the city's leading musical groups and Lee as an impresario-conductor to be reckoned with.

By this time Lee had the run of the Shaw house and was quickly becoming the centre around which the whole household revolved. He gave his lessons there, using the upstairs reception room for the choral and instrumental rehearsals which, far from annoying the neighbours, delighted them (according to Shaw) because of the high standard achieved.

And why, one may wonder, did Lee not teach

and rehearse in his own more commodious house around in Harrington Street?

The explanation appears to be this. His mother, who lived with him and his younger brother, was, like Charles II, an unconscionable time a-dying. Her death notice (March 1860) mentions a 'protracted illness'. Since she died at fifty-five the protracted illness sounds like cancer. But whatever it was it would have put music-making in the house out of the question, so some other venue had to be found. The six-month period of mourning for her would have made music-making no less inappropriate. Then there was the ailing younger brother, whose death in May 1862 so shattered Lee that a friend had to be set to watch him in case he attempted suicide.

There is also mention of an irascible housekeeper in Harrington Street who seems to have been able to drive away pupils without getting the sack from her master.

All in all Bessie's house was the solution to these problems, providing Lee with a most acceptable professional and personal refuge. It would also gratify Bessie, filling her life with pleasant activity in congenial company.

Lee's teaching theories had been brought together into a course of tuition which Bessie and her household respectfully referred to as the Method. It gave her, says her son, a cause and a creed which filled a life that would otherwise have been empty and pointless. The Method was based upon Lee's observations of the best singers who came within his hearing, and upon his dissection of birds' throats, together with scraps of pathological information picked up from anatomists. It called for up to four years of tuition, but the expenditure of time and effort was rewarded by the ability to produce pure tone without undue strain. The Method also preserved the voice. Shaw claimed that his mother continued to be able to produce pure tone into her eighties, presumably without undue effort. He subjected himself to the Method, but his teacher was his mother, not Lee. Nevertheless he too continued to sing into his nineties, not publicly of course, but for his own satisfaction and the nocturnal delectation of his wife.

Shaw's attitude to the Method did not remain consistent throughout his life. In his music critic period he occasionally made snide references to singing teachers and their theories, sarcastically dismissing those who claimed to have rediscovered Porpora's lost method. In his play *Caesar and Cleopatra* there is a minor character, the Musician, who sounds very like a satirical sketch of Lee: 'Assuredly I and no one else can teach the Queen . . . All the other teachers are quacks: I have exposed them repeatedly.' But this would have been a reminiscence of the London Lee. When later on he wrote about the Dublin Lee it was from his Dublin view of him as a choice and master spirit.

We have no detailed account of how the Method worked. An allusion by Shaw indicates that it included making the normally involuntary use of pharyngeal muscles a voluntary process. But we haven't much more than this, nor does Lee's book *The Voice* take us any further.

This book, *The Voice: its Artistic Production, Development, and Preservation*, was published in Dublin at the end of 1869 by M'Glashan and Gill, acting in concert with Simpkin, Marshall & Co. of London. It is a handsomely produced volume, expensively bound and lavish in its use of gilt. The price of 3s. 6d. (17½p.) for cloth binding and 5s. (25p.) for full calf is so uneconomic as to suggest that Lee may have subsidised M'Glashan and Gill's costs, intending it, with its plethora of anatomical illustrations pinched from another M'Glashan and Gill publication, to be more of a brochure to lure prospective pupils to so profoundly learned a teacher than a treatise for the genuine student.

Shaw tells us what is self-evidently true: that although Lee's name is on the title page he wasn't the real author. The book was written, he says, by a scamp of a derelict doctor. The doctor is not named but we can confidently if not with absolute certainty identify him as Dr Malachi Kilgarriff, a demonstrator in anatomy and Lee's next-door neighbour in Harrington Street. At the presumed time of the book's being written, Kilgarriff was prevented by illness from working at the anatomy school and may have been very glad to 'ghost' for Lee. But although he may have appeared a derelict scamp to the supercilious eye of the thirteen-year-old Shaw, he was in fact an eminently respectable and well-qualified physician, later a consultant at the Mater Hosptial with a private practice in Harcourt Street, nearly opposite the house in which Shaw *père et fils* would soon be lodging after being abandoned by Bessie.

There is one more relevant fact about Kilgarriff. He was a Catholic.

Lee, within a couple of years of his brother's death in 1862, had evidently reached agreement with Bessie, and presumably with her husband, to move in with the Shaws completely. The arrangement, to be convenient, required removal to larger premises. Lee's own house was certainly larger than the Shaws', but for them to have moved in with him, giving the appearance of becoming his lodgers, would smack of *lèse majesté*. It would also create gossip — perhaps one should say *more* gossip. And this is assuming that Lee would not have been anxious to get away from a house in which his mother and brother had died.

To move to a more fashionable area was obviously desirable. To the Shaws this would be a step nearer to their proper place of residence as members of a baronetted family. To Lee it had professional advantages: a good address attracted genteel pupils. Joseph Robinson lived in Upper Fitzwilliam Street in a house of £64 valuation; presently he would find himself a neighbour of Sir Robert P. Stewart whose house had a valuation of £80. Such residences were wildly beyond the financial reach of the Shaws, and also beyond the combined reach of them and Lee. In the event they were able to achieve No. 1 Hatch Street (valuation £35), a corner house half of which was in quite fashionable Lower Leeson Street. The Lord Chancellor lived a few yards across the way, and Leeson Street neighbours included judges and the senior partner of Guinness's Brewery, Sir Arthur himself, great-grandson of the original Arthur Guinness. Indeed Leeson Street was named after a brewer, Joseph Leeson, later Earl of Milltown.

This is an opportune moment to consider GCS's finances at that period. It is most unlikely he had more than £5 a week, and may not have had even that much. Shaw generally refers to Clibborn & Shaw as if it was GCS's firm, in which George Clibborn hovered spectrally in the background. The truth was the reverse. GCS's modest £500 investment left him the small boy in the concern. In practical terms he may have been little more than chief clerk, his salary supplemented by a share of the profits, if any. Harvest failure was no uncommon thing in Ireland, and such failures must have meant lean times for corn merchants and their mills. Taking one year with another, the profits would hardly have been luscious.

Moreover, GCS's share of the profits looks to have

been small in relation to Clibborn's. GCS died virtually
penniless. When George Clibborn died sixteen years later he left the goodly sum of £9,074. 14s. 9d. And this wasn't because he lived in humbler style than his partner did, for Clibborn's house, No. 10 Upper Leeson Street, had a valuation of £39. The notion therefore presents itself that since GCS, timid, unenterprising, not always sober, was unlikely to have been a satisfactory partner, Clibborn may have had to do the lion's share of the work, thus feeling morally justified in so arranging the firm's accounts that he could quietly pocket the lion's share of the takings. The oddest feature of the partnership is that neither on GCS's death in 1885 nor on Clibborn's in 1901, when the business was disposed of by Mrs Clibborn, was GCS's £500 investment returned to his family. Mrs Clibborn may have appropriated the proceeds of the sale for herself in good faith, believing the firm to have been entirely her late husband's property. It isn't so easy to give Clibborn the benefit of such a doubt. On his partner's death he seems to have told GCS's brother, Uncle Frederick of the Valuation Office, who was looking after the affairs of the deceased, that the firm had come to grief. This is what Uncle Frederick reported to Bessie and her son in London. In view of the fact that the firm survived GCS by sixteen years, at the expiry of which it could still find a purchaser, and above all in view of Clibborn's £9,074, we have good reason to believe that GCS and his heirs were cheated by his partner.

4

Sonny Shaw grew up in a house irradiated by the sunshine of music under the mesmeric Lee, with, occasionally, a different kind of enlivening from the visits of the Rabelaisian Gurly uncle who would return from his voyages with an extended repertoire of dirty limericks. But everything was liable to be clouded suddenly by his father's outbursts of alcoholic rage, brief but alarming, in which GCS might dash ornaments from the mantelpiece. But he stopped short at striking anyone. His son believed his timidity made forbearance habitual with him. Life at Dalkey, however, in Torca Cottage, which Lee rented for the summer months, was more pleasant and relaxed.

St John Ervine quotes in his biography a 1907 letter in which Shaw admits that in other eyes Dalkey might appear no more than a quite ordinary and insipid seaside place, but that to him as a child it had been wonderland. From Torca Hill there are splendid views of the wide sweep of Dublin Bay, which enthusiastic jackeens used to be fond of comparing to the Bay of Naples, the greatest enthusiasm being generated in the bosoms of those jackeens who had never been next or near Naples. But Neapolitan or not, Dalkey accustomed Shaw to scenes of natural beauty and to the physical freedom of roaming around at will, bathing at White Rock in stimulatingly chilly water, and omitting Sunday church. For the family had given up attending church on going out to Dalkey and did not resume it on returning to Hatch Street.

Amongst Shaw's other Dalkey achievements was setting fire to the gorse on the hill and passing the blame to another boy, and getting himself nicknamed Bullockshop through boasting that the Shaws always had *real* meat in their stew.

For a while the Shaws and Lee had as a Torca neighbour a little dumpling of a man whose use of a monocle caused him to be known as the Major. He was Richard Pigott, yet another Catholic, then supplementing a lean income from the publication of a patriotic newspaper with the privy sale of porno-

graphic photographs taken by himself. Later, in a
[34] desperate attempt to provide his adored sons with
the education of gentlemen, he became the forger
of the Parnell letters. He was erroneously believed
by Shaw to have taken the well-known group photograph of Lee and his friends. I have an original
mounted print which shows it to have been taken
by Millard and Robinson of Sackville (O'Connell)
Street.

While living in Torca Cottage, the young Shaw was
sent to a preparatory school in nearby Glasthule,
conducted by one William Halpin. The school doesn't
appear to have made any deep impression on him,
for good or ill. He was to recall with cold dislike his
next school, the Wesleyan Connexional in St Stephen's
Green, a place chosen for him not because his parents
had any predilection for Methodism but because it
was the nearest genteel Protestant school to Hatch
Street. His sojourn at the Central Model School we
have already dealt with. It ended when his father,
sympathising with the boy's flat refusal to return for
another term with the sons of Catholic tradesmen,
insisted that he be transferred to the undeniably
Protestant Dublin English Scientific and Commercial
Day School. This was conducted in Aungier Street
by the Incorporated Society for Promoting English
Protestant Schools in Ireland.

Since Lee had been responsible for having Shaw
sent to the Central Model, holding that the teaching
there was better than at the Wesleyan establishment,
the boy's removal to Aungier Street at his father's
insistence represents the sole recorded rebuff to the
cuckoo in the nest by the nest's lawful head.

McNulty alleged that Shaw presented himself at
Aungier Street in 'an Eton jacket, knickerbockers,
long stockings and laced-up boots'. Shaw denied this
allegation, but not another one that during a game of

schoolyard cricket he bowled McNulty a ball in such a way that on being hit it flashed backwards and smashed a stained glass window in the Carmelite church on the other side of the laneway. Whereupon Shaw threw himself on the ground and rolled around, screaming with glee. The Prior, Rev. Spratt, proved to be unexpectedly kindly and understanding about the incident. McNulty doesn't mention who paid for the damage, but the chances are that the Incorporated Society did the gentlemanly thing.

Before he was quite fourteen years of age Shaw was sent by Bessie to be interviewed for a job with a wholesale woollen merchants, Scott, Spain & Rooney of Merchants Quay. The junior partner was willing to take him on, but the senior said he was too young and too unfitted for the work and sent him home again. For which Shaw was afterwards to express heartfelt gratitude. But at fifteen he was propelled from the nest once more to get a job. This time he was successful, his Uncle Frederick having prepared the way for him at the office of Charles Uniacke Townshend, land agent and civil engineer, 15 Molesworth Street. The year 1871 accordingly saw Shaw working as an office boy at a salary of £18 a year.

Townshend was the seventh son of Thomas Townshend, member of the family seated at Myross Wood, Co. Cork. These Townshends were cousins of the Townshends of nearby Derry House, Rosscarbery, the head of which branch, Horace (sometimes Horatio), had added Payne to his surname in accordance with the will of one Thomas Payne of Edstaston House, Wem, Shropshire, on succeeding to that estate in right of his wife. Horace Payne-Townshend had two daughters, the elder of whom, Charlotte Frances, was to marry Shaw twenty-seven years later.

Horace's ancestors had been settled in Rosscarbery since the end of the seventeenth century, and Horace loved his Cork home. But the Englishwoman he had married hated it, and the Irish along with it. In time she came to despise Horace and, being extremely strongwilled, led him a dog's life. Eventually she was able to do what she liked, telling him one day that she was taking a house in Dublin for the season, to which she proposed carrying off her teenage daughters. This wasn't altogether wilfulness on her part. There was something in it of the Victorian mother's desire to float her girls in polite society with a view to netting eligible husbands. Mrs Payne-Townshend and her daughters were therefore in their Merrion Square house at a period in the 1870s when Oscar Wilde was living with his parents on the opposite side of the Square and Shaw was working in Townshend's office in nearby Molesworth Street and living about half a mile away in Hatch Street. It is probable that Shaw had at least a distant know-ledge of Charlotte in Dublin, and may even have seen her there when she was eighteen or nineteen.

Shaw's office companions were articled apprentices or clerks, sons of gentlemen and university men. Although as office boy he was of lower rank, he seems to have mixed with them on equal terms, joining them — or perhaps it was they who joined him — in impromptu performances of scenes from Italian opera. Sometimes Townshend walked in on these performances but took no disciplinary action. His only recorded venture in this line was to take Shaw aside on overhearing him argue about religion with one of the apprentices and make him promise never to mention religion again while on the premises. Shaw reluctantly gave the undertaking, and said it troubled his conscience for the rest of his life.

We hear of his being put out of countenance by his

companions on at least two occasions. Once, he was accused of not knowing what a syllogism was, where- upon he hurried off to a dictionary and discovered that like Monsieur Jourdain with prose he had been using syllogisms for years without realising it. The other put-down was when a clerk remarked that every youth thought of himself as a great man, which brought Shaw face to face with the realisation that he had been making just this very assumption about himself too.

5

Not alone did Shaw attend Lee's domestic rehearsals and public concerts and performances of opera as a matter of course, he also went to the theatre. In Dublin he saw Henry Irving, then on the threshhold of celebrity, as Digby Grant in Albery's *Two Roses*. Also in the audience was another Dublin youth, Bram Stoker, future author of *Dracula*, but in 1871 much more stagestruck than Shaw and already a worshipper of Irving. A quarter of a century later in London, Stoker and Shaw would cross pens with no little heat on the subject of Irving's genius. Shaw and Stoker also saw performances by Barry Sullivan, a leader of the pre-Irving school and famous for his Macbeth and his Richard III. Shaw professed to admire Sullivan more than Irving, but one is left with the suspicion that he was using Sullivan as a stick to beat the other man. Shaw had reason to dislike and resent Henry Irving, as we shall see.

Shaw's artistic inclinations at this time were not towards drama or music but art. His ambition was to follow in the footsteps of Michaelangelo, to which end he enrolled himself at the Royal Dublin Society's drawing school. After some lessons he asked McNulty to pose for him in the nude. McNulty declined, partly, one gathers, from shyness, partly from fear of catching cold in the Hatch Street top floor bedroom. But McNulty was quite willing to accompany him on frequent visits to the recently opened National Gallery in Merrion Square. In retrospect Shaw came to regard these visits as constituting a most important part of his education, acknowledging the debt by making the Gallery heir to one-third of his fortune. Drama, in the shape of the Royal Academy of Dramatic Art, in London, received another third, the remainder going to the British Library. Thus music, the greatest artistic influence of all on him and the great love of his life (and the subject of the last article he was to publish), was left out of his will.

Shaw took the constant domestic supply of music in Hatch Street so much for granted that he didn't bother to learn the piano or even his notes. It is a measure of Bessie's neglect of her obviously musical son that she hadn't taught him or got him taught. Her chief concern in this area was the musical development of her eldest daughter. Lee was encouraged to teach Lucy the piano, and it was from this time onward, said Shaw, that her dislike of Lee was apparent. Lee also trained her voice, repeating his success with the mother and leaving both of them with the conviction that a great future as a professional singer lay before Lucy.

As for the other sister, Yuppy, her consolation was to be her mother's favourite, perhaps because she had more of the Gurly colouring than the others, perhaps because she was the least robust of the three. Shaw seems to have been the outsider in the home. Bessie was no son worshipper, and for once the Irish maternal tradition of exalting the son above the daughters was not observed. He had little or no companionable contact with parents or sisters and was too young for any real companionship with Lee or with his Gurly Uncle Walter, well disposed though these were towards him. Occasionally there were little kindly gestures by other grown ups. For instance, the musician Joseph Robinson loaned him illustrated books so that he could study the pictures. Uncles and aunts there was no lack of, their children providing him with a further host of cousins, but there was little social contact. An exception was his Aunt Emily (who 'exceeded in nothing but snuff') and her husband Rev. Carroll, he who had officiated at Bessie's wedding and who in baptising Shaw had ordered the sexton to stand in as godfather in the absence of the official appointee. The baptism had been performed in Carroll's church, St Bride's, and must have been one of the very few occasions on which the building was of any practical use. For it was situated in one of the poorest and most Catholic areas in the old city, leaving Carroll with little or no flock. But he conscientiously struggled to keep the doomed church in repair, compiled its history and availed himself of the independence his Rector's freehold gave him to launch pamphlets against the lord chancellor on the subject of education. St Bride's was demolished in 1898, thirteen years after Carroll's death. Its organ is preserved in the National Museum. Carroll also wrote antiquarian articles for the *Freeman's Journal*, a recognised organ of Catholicism, and this, together with his Fenian sympathies and priest-like garb, caused him to be known as 'Father' Carroll. The fact that his Shaw in-laws were harbouring a Catholic in their household did not oblige such a man to break off relations. But this was not the case with other members of the clan.

Naturally Shaw didn't attribute the family boycott of the Hatch Street *ménage* to Lee's Catholicism. He blamed his father's drunkenness, explaining that drink made his father socially unbearable by making him morose instead of jovial. In the pre-joint-household days GCS and his family had been invited to musical parties in Bushy Park, seat of the bachelor second baronet. The setting up of the joint household was to end all that. On the baronet's death in 1869 (Shaw being thirteen), GCS and the family called to Bushy Park to pay their respects. Shaw was to remember the coffin lying in state in the hall, and that was to be his last glimpse of the interior of the family seat. There were two reasons. The new baronet, the Recorder, preferred to remain in his own home, Kimmage Manor, and let Bushy Park to a tenant. The other reason was that while in theory he was all for religious toleration, and could vote for the municipal reform that enabled Daniel O'Connell to be elected Lord Mayor of Dublin (the first Catholic to hold the office since the Battle of the Boyne), in practice he placed social barriers between himself and all Catholics. Macaulay was to denounce him as a bigot. Sir Frederick did not have to explain in so many words why he was dropping the Hatch Street Shaws, but drop them he did, and the other Shaws took their lead from the head of the family. It would have caused the Recorder deep grief to know that after his death his beloved Kimmage Manor would be acquired by a Catholic religious order, the Holy Ghost Fathers.

We are told, however, that after the departure to London of Lee and Bessie, the decontaminated GCS was received back into the fold.

The break up of the *ménage* was not caused by a rupture in the relationship between Lee and the Shaws, but by a clash between Lee and Sir Robert Prescott Stewart. Shaw rightly described Lee as the target of academic hostility in Dublin. Stewart, the chief academic, probably took little notice of Lee so long as Lee was merely operating on a modest scale with frankly amateur forces. It was another story when Lee began to muscle in on activities which Stewart regarded as proper only to academically qualified professionals like himself. Lee's Leeson Street neighbour, Sir Arthur Guinness, had with his brother (later Lord Iveagh) financed a series of Dublin Exhibitions on the lines of the famous Dargan Exhibition of 1853, itself inspired by the London event of 1851. Lee must have called around to Sir Arthur at the right time because he obtained the privilege of organising the gala concert which inaugurated the proceedings for the 1872 Exhibition. In spite of Lee's technical shortcomings the concert was entirely successful. This would have made it clear to Stewart that Lee had to be stopped as a matter of urgency. So for the 1873 concert, for which Stewart was commissioned to compose an inaugural ode, a spanner was thrown in the works. Lee had assumed command at the rehearsals as a matter of course but seems to have made so many technical errors that Stewart humiliated him by openly correcting them, undermining Lee's authority with the Amateur Musical Society. Stewart went further. He insisted on taking over the job of conducting the ode and, being the most accomplished musical technician in the country, can only have impressed the chorus as being vastly the superior of their official conductor. The seasoned warriors of the orchestra would long before have rumbled Lee in those areas in which he was chancing his arm.

The sequel justified Stewart's arrogant note in the margin of his copy of the Theatre Royal history: 'I unmasked one arrant impostor and drove him from Dublin.'

Within a few days the bitterly humiliated Lee had packed his bags and left Dublin, and we have no record of his ever again having set foot in the city, or indeed in Ireland. London, or rather a tiny part of it,

was to be his sphere of action for the remainder of his
life. He had long planned to go to London and
conquer it as he was conquering Dublin, but at a time
of his own choosing. He hadn't reckoned on his
departure being the graceless and premature flight
it turned out to be. Only eighteen months previously
he had renewed for a long term his Torca Cottage
tenancy; he had just renamed his society the New
Philharmonic and had founded the National Institute
of Music. He was also in the midst of plans for another
big concert. Only a burning sense of shame could
have made him abandon everything he had built up in
Dublin in the way he did.

Shaw was seventeen at the time and simply cannot
have been unaware of the debacle. Yet although in
garrulous moments he was to let slip many a detail of
his Dublin family life that he would have preferred
to keep to himself, no word ever escaped him either
of Lee's Catholicism or of his humiliation at Stewart's
hands. Another humiliation awaited Shaw himself.
Within a month his mother had packed her bags too,
and with Yuppy had followed Lee to London. Bessie
was insensitive as to the date of her desertion of her
husband and son: 17 June 1873, her twenty-first
wedding anniversary.

Shaw was to claim that at least a year or more
passed between Lee's departure and his mother's. But
the evidence of the mail boat's passenger lists is con-
clusive. Bessie had hot-footed it after 'her man', as
Shaw described Lee in a candid moment. There is
always the possibility that Bessie, in following Lee to
London with a daughter as chaperone, merely wanted
to coax him back to Dublin, Hatch Street posing too
much of a financial problem without his contribution.
The fact remains that when Lee's departure took on
the aspect of finality, Bessie elected to join him. She
returned the following March (1874) to tidy up her

affairs in Dublin, concluding the Hatch Street tenancy, selling off the furniture (except for the [43] piano), and placing husband and son in 'comforable bachelor lodgings' in No. 61 Harcourt Street.

The change, said Shaw, seemed to be a great relief to GCS. His financial burdens were reduced, and there was a blessed freedom from the cuckoo in the nest. This, however, doesn't altogether square with the more or less contemporary sketch which Shaw had drafted for the eyes of that 'chère madame' (see page 22), in which the deserted father's distress is mocked at so unpleasantly. Nor does it take account of GCS's feelings at his wife's humiliating treatment of him, nor of his shaming descent from the grandeur of Hatch Street and a summer retreat in Dalkey to 'bachelor lodgings' in Harcourt Street. The abruptness and completeness of the family break-up must have made the experience truly traumatic for both father and son. But people have to adjust themselves to altered circumstances. GCS continued to go to the Jervis Street office and to the Commercial Buildings in Dame Street where McNulty used see him seated at a window, spectacles well down on his nose, reading the financial papers. Shaw continued at Townshends, where he had already achieved unexpected advancement. The cashier, discovered pilfering, took himself off and the sixteen-year-old Shaw was appointed stopgap cashier. He was found efficient enough to be left in the job at a doubled salary. The promotion must have been soothing. The added responsibility was certainly welcome as it increased his self-respect. The ledgers disciplined his handwriting, changing it from a sloping scrawl to an upright script, legible though minute, and said to have been modelled on that of his predecessor.

With the cessation of the almost daily musicmaking

he had become accustomed to, he set about filling the gap in his life by teaching himself the piano. This he did by propping a piano score of *Don Giovanni* in front of him and experimentally arranging his fingers on various notes until the result produced the overture's unmistakeable opening chord. In the absence of natural talent for the keyboard, such self-tuition failed to make him a good pianist and a confident sightreader, but as was the case with his self-taught shorthand, while he never was in full command of the medium he mastered enough of it for his purposes.

Meanwhile the friendship with McNulty became closer, and when McNulty was transferred to the Newry branch of the Bank of Ireland, of which he was an official all his working life, the friends exchanged confidential letters almost daily, some of these embodying playlets or snatches of dialogue. As a celebrity Shaw became worried about these letters, in case there was anything in them he would not care to be made public either before or after his death. He accordingly asked McNulty to destroy every letter he had kept. McNulty, it transpired, had kept them all, or at any rate a great number of them, and, although he knew they were worth a fortune, carried them into his back garden and had a bonfire. A bonfire, it may be added, the very thought of which will cause Shaw biographers of the future — and there will be many — to wring their hands in anguish. A fragment of what is claimed to be an 1876 letter to McNulty is published in Vol. I of the *Collected Letters*.

Close as the bond was between Shaw and McNulty it might have been even closer. McNulty fell in love with Lucy and proposed. She gently refused, explaining that her being his senior by three years made a marriage between them imprudent. McNulty, for a North of Ireland man (and a bank official) remained oddly sentimental about her, declaring, even when married and with a family, that she was still the love of his life and the most beautiful girl he had ever known. She for her part wrote to him every week. He treasured her letters but, without any request from her, made a bonfire of them after her death, remarking that 'There are some things too sacred for print.' In her concise and very businesslike will (drawn up by herself) Lucy left McNulty her Bechstein piano, its seat and a music cabinet. She directed that these were to be delivered to him in Dublin, adding with characteristic Shavian considerateness, 'carriage paid'.

6

To return to the Harcourt Street lodgers. Shaw had developed another friendship, with Chichester Bell, a cousin of the inventor of the telephone. He studied Italian with him without learning it, and read the works of the Carlow born scientist, John Tyndall, then enjoying a great vogue, his lecture in Belfast in 1874 to the British Association having aroused tremendous controversy. He also took lessons in playing the cornet from George Kennedy, a member of the Theatre Royal band who used also play for Lee. He abandoned the cornet on learning that his lip wasn't suitable. There was the occasional family funeral — 'prodigies of black pomp' he called them. These generally took place to Mount Jerome, formerly a Shaw estate but a cemetery from 1836, the secretary of which was his paternal Aunt Charlotte's husband. This gentleman brought Shaw on a tour of the sepulchral horrors in his domain, and if we were never to believe any other word uttered by Shaw we can readily accept his assurance that the experience converted him to the practice of crem-

ation.

In the spring of 1875 the popular preaching team of Moody and Sankey visited Dublin, drawing from Shaw the satirical letter to *Public Opinion*, an English news magazine, notable as his first appearance in print. To his more pious relations the letter could only be interpreted as an open profession of atheism.

The following year, 1876, was to be his last as an inhabitant of his native land. Townshend had evidently had no intention of leaving Shaw in so important a post as that of cashier, for he brought a nephew into the office, making him cashier and assigning so few duties to Shaw that he was to all intents and purposes being given notice. In the event he went before he was told to go. On 29 February he formally notified Townshend that he would be discontinuing his services from the end of March.

Before March was out Yuppy had died from tuberculosis at Ventnor in the Isle of Wight, whither she had been sent in the hope that the mild climate would save her. At the end of March, his employment concluded, Shaw, aged nineteen years and nine months, his worldly goods in a carpet bag, boarded the mail boat. Some twenty-two hours later he arrived in London on a beautiful April day. He wasn't to see Ireland again for thirty years, and even then it would be only at his wife's insistence.

3
London

In his later years Shaw maintained that his move to
London was the logical step of advancing upon the
great centre of English literature where he intended
to be king one day. In his imagery Shaw the auto-
cratic democrat tended to view himself as a king in
the republic of art. One doubts whether anything
of this nature was in his mind as he got off the train
at Euston and entered a cab to be driven with his
bags to his mother's home, No. 13 Victoria (sub-
sequently Netherton) Grove, off the Fulham Road.
During the drive he cannot but have been bewildered
by the scale of London in comparison with Dublin.

He was aware as a matter of general knowledge
that London was the world's largest city. Dickens
had given him vivid impressions of its atmosphere
and of the colourful characters who inhabited it. But
no amount of reading and theoretical knowledge
would have prepared a highly susceptible Dublin
youth for the overwhelming impact of the reality.
Dublin had an ascertainable central point, Nelson
Pillar in Sackville (now O'Connell) Street. A few
minutes walk from the Pillar brought you to Trinity
College and the head office of the Bank of Ireland,
the Custom House, the Four Courts, the cathedrals,
the theatres, recital rooms, the Castle (seat of government and official residence of the viceroy), the

fashionable shops of Grafton Street and the nest of side streets in which merchants had their offices. Ten minutes on foot from the Pillar brought you to the select semi-suburban residential areas, twenty minutes in a cab brought you to deserted bathing strands or to the open country. In short, in the Dublin of the 1870s man was still master of the urban situation. In the vastness of London the individual person became its slave. Shaw was never to feel at home there.

There were other differences apparent to the novice Londoner. Londoners were more sprucely dressed than Dubliners, they walked more briskly and purposefully, their expressions were more cheerful and good humoured, yet you didn't find the same tendency in Londoners to stop on the footpath for a long leisurely chat that was so noticeable a feature of life in the city Shaw had just left. And there were fewer beggars, less shabbiness in the public buildings. Above all London gave no impression whatsoever of being, like Dublin, a city long past its prime. It was vibrantly and fully alive.

Shaw left no account of how he was received when he arrived at Victoria Grove. The Shaws, he always insisted, were completely undemonstrative, although the heartiness of his own welcome to friends and the open and frank cordiality of his manner belied this in his own case. Nevertheless that family reunion in April 1876 must have been an embarrassing and awkward affair, none of the parties being sure of what to say or to do, as is the rule when families are not nomadic and therefore inexperienced in dealing with departures and returns. But there need be no doubt that the chief topic of conversation was Yuppy's death. Shaw himself remarked in a general way that death always makes us human for a little while, and in *The Unsocial Socialist* he describes the phenomenon of a husband shedding tears over the corpse of his wife while being aware that in his heart there was no real grief, no true sense of bereavement. Elsewhere he was to write of that curious feeling of relief one experiences when a relation or a friend dies, as of being finished and done with them at last. Mrs Shaw was for her part more conventionally emotional than her son would have us believe. Lucy's Dublin friend Constance Shaw (no relation) told how when Mrs Shaw had Constance to herself one day she indulged in a burst of bitter tears, complaining that her children didn't love her. She seems to have made a habit of this. McNulty relates how he himself had a very similar experience with her.

Lucy and her brother went to Ventnor to visit poor Yuppy's grave, marking the event by having a studio photograph taken of themselves by a local photographer. Their demeanour was quite Shavian: in the photograph two more placid and unconcerned mourners you never did see.

What Shaw's financial situation was during his first days in London he does not tell us. It is probable that he had arrived with relatively substantial savings, something of the order of £25 or even £30. The photographs of him at that time show him genteely suited, and the Ventnor photograph shows him the possessor of a highly respectable bowler hat. Moreover, three years after his arrival he had a guinea or so to spare for another studio photograph, the most successful to date. The unpleasant sneer that disfigured his face in the photograph taken with Edward McNulty in Dublin has been replaced by dignity and self-possession, and for the first time one can discern the outlines of the famous face of the future. Neither the expression nor what we can see of the clothing suggests dire poverty.

2

[50] His first three months in London were given over to sightseeing, doing the round of museums and galleries, acquiring a pedestrian's knowledge of London's topography, and sending epistolary reports back to McNulty. Some of his evenings were spent at Lee's quarters in 13 Park Lane, accompanying at the rehearsals of the various music groups and occasionally drafting publicity paragraphs for the papers.

Since Park Lane was one of the best possible addresses in London, Lee's occupancy of a house there might indicate his Caesarean conquest of London, a conquest more thorough than he had made of Dublin. But this picture needs correction. For one thing, No. 13 Park Lane was only part of a house, needing No. 14 to complete the original design. It was, therefore, small for a Park Lane mansion, and was situated in the dark, narrow, unfashionable end of the thoroughfare, though it had a fine music room. (The house was blitzed during the Second World War.)

No. 13 Park Lane had another disadvantage. Two years before Lee moved in it had been the scene of a murder. The tenant, a Madame Rial, was strangled in the kitchen by her housekeeper, and it came out during the trial that titled gentlemen (including the then Earl of Lucan) used to visit Madame and leave her gifts of money. The house was therefore probably going very cheap by Park Lane standards. Lee had rented it from Julian Marshall, an enthusiast for tennis and for music, a contributor to *Grove's Dictionary of Music and Musicians* and a collector who could boast of having in his possession the sketchbook in which Beethoven drafted parts of the Pastoral Symphony. Marshall was also a director of Simpkin, Marshall & Co., joint publishers with M'Glashan and Gill of *The Voice*, and it was to him

that Lee had sold for £300 in 1874 his interest in
Torca Cottage.

We learn from Shaw's letter to his mother, written
when he was still in Dublin, that only a year after
settling in Park Lane Lee was declaring he was ruined,
Shaw's comment being that during his experience
of Lee he had heard the same complaint some three
hundred and sixty-five times a year. The truth is that
Lee's status in London was nothing like that which he
had in Dublin. He enjoyed a brief vogue as a fashionable teacher but seems to have devoted much energy
to organising concerts and opera productions for the
amusement of lady and gentlemen amateurs. But the
London papers did not report these occasions as
extensively as the Dublin papers had done, not even
when Lee organised a charity concert in the house of
Lord Londonderry, a sumptuous Italianate palace
which was only a few yards away from Lee's own
home.

Nevertheless, Shaw kept fairly close to Lee during
those first few years in London, partly no doubt
because of the attraction of the music-making, partly
because of the opportunities to enlarge his London
acquaintance, partly because Lee was making every
effort to get congenial work for him. Lee seems to
have noticed that Shaw had a facility with the pen for
not only did he get him to draft brochures and
publicity paragraphs but tried hard to get openings
for him as a critic and writer on music. Indeed it was
Lee who got Shaw his first foothold on the ladder of
London journalism. Lee had become acquainted with
a Captain Donald Shaw (no relation) who was editing
a little magazine called *The Hornet*. He accepted the
post of music critic and got Shaw to ghost the articles
for him. In return Shaw got all, or part of, the
proceeds, a thing which slipped his memory when
calculating the paltry sum he earned by his pen during

his first nine years in London. To the six odd pounds
he stated as the total, there must be added his *Hornet*
earnings which at the very least amounted to £20.
Then there were occasional small sums given him by
Lee for expenses incurred as Lee's publicity agent;
later on Lee was to offer him a commission to
re-write *The Voice* for a London edition.

Some biographers allege that after his first three
months of bed and board with his mother, Lucy
urged her to sling him out to fend for himself. St
John Ervine, who without ever having met Lucy or
Bessie grew to detest them, saw this as unwarranted
victimisation by a daughter who was herself batten-
ing on her mother just as much as the son was. It is
quite possible, quite likely in fact, that in the ups
and downs of domestic life and of a woman's biology,
Lucy may have let fly at the brother who to all
appearances intended to go on consuming without
producing. But that Lucy deliberately and cold-
bloodedly asked that her brother be thrown into
the gutter is totally at variance with all that we know
of her and of her relations with him.

Nevertheless, it was inevitable that some kind of
pressure would have been put on him to Do Something. He did. We know that he went to at least four
interviews in London which had been set up for him
by friends back in Ireland. But when he answered
advertisements the replies that survive suggest that as
a candidate for conventional employment he seemed
more concerned with literary self-expression than
with actually landing the job. The fact seems to be
that the writing of the criticisms for *The Hornet*
made him aware at last that nature had equipped
him for authorship. But he still failed to take up
nature's specific hints that he try dramatic authorship. She had nudged him in his teens towards the
writing of a play about the domesticity of the Holy

Family, the Virgin Mother being characterised as a shrew. Then there had been the little dialogue written for that *chère madame.* But these were only unfinished and formless scraps. His first full-scale literary work was a novel. It was begun in the spring of 1879, he being twenty-three, and its title was *Immaturity.*

Immaturity is a study of immaturity by an immature author, which is its strength and its weakness. After exhuming it from that literary necropolis which prolific authors maintain in their home when they have not used the crematorium of the fireplace, Shaw found that mice had nibbled away the edges of the manuscript. This gave him the opening to boast that not even the mice had been able to finish it. Not many Shavians are likely to have finished it either, at least not without much skipping. The cast of characters is headed by Robert Smith who, it goes without saying where a first novel by a twenty-three-year-old is concerned, is a self-portrait. St John Ervine, not the least perceptive of Shaw's biographers, put his finger on a revealing passage in the novel. Robert Smith has begun to crave for a female friend who will cheer him up in his depressed moments as he struggles along the thorny way to 'truth and human perfection':

> Happily, he found none such. The power to stand alone is worth acquiring at the expense of much sorrowful soltitude.

Here Shaw is echoing Ibsen before he had read Ibsen, whose Dr Stockmann in *The Enemy of the People* discovers at the end of the play that the strongest man is he who stands alone, and that he who confronts the public on a point of moral principle should not risk wearing his good trousers while so doing. It was part of Shaw's immaturity that, like another and earlier Ibsen character, he was waving aloft the banner of ideals like 'stand alone' and 'search for Truth and Human Perfection'. Such slogans have a heroic ring which induce complacent feelings in the person uttering them. They also have a highly convenient flexibility of application, for it did not take a great degree of self-deception to convince yet another Ibsen character, Hjalmar Ekdal in *The Wild Duck*, that to lie down on the sofa every day after lunch, while Mrs Ekdal carried on with the work, was a most practical way of conducting his own search for Truth and Human Perfection.

Not that any charge against Shaw of idleness or laziness can stick. His 'scriptoral industry' (as he called it) was carried almost to a fault, in sickness and in health, until death did him part from his pen in his ninety-fifth year. But a charge of sometimes waving aloft a banner just for the sake of waving aloft a banner might be more difficult to dispose of.

A charge against Shaw's mother of not being a reasonably capable and economical housewife might also be difficult to dispose of, assuming that a woman should possess these qualities. When Shaw, always unable to resist a joke at his own expense, said that he hadn't thrown himself into the struggle for existence but had thrown his mother into it, many complacently chose to accept this as a literal truth. But nothing we know of Bessie allows us to believe she would have allowed herself to be thrown anywhere by anyone. She wasn't the only mother in the world who went out to work to support her family. She had a small income, probably about £40, from the Whitcroft legacy, which she supplemented by teaching singing to private pupils and, later, by training the girls' choir at the North London Collegiate School. And she doesn't appear to have made her son's domestic situation so unbearable as to prevent him from writing five pages of *Immaturity* a day, and, if he missed a day, doing a double stint the day after.

Immaturity, begun in March 1879, was completed
by the following September. A week later he was
drafting a kind of *curriculum vitae*, obviously intended for a prospective employer, for Commerce had
reared its unwelcome head again, and again on the
prompting of a well-wishing relation. This was a
cousin, a woman novelist of some contemporary
success, married to Cashel Hoey, agent-general for
Victoria. Her victim must have doubly damned her
interference, for more literary genius has been
blighted by such benevolence than by lack of
perception in publishers. Cousin Fanny introduced
him to the manager of the Edison Telephone Company of London, Arnold White. The result was a
job in the right-of-way department in which he was
to be 'instructed in the profession of a telephone
engineer' but was in fact sent around London's
East End to persuade householders to allow telephone posts to be erected on their premises. The
salary was £48 a year. In other words he was at
twenty-three picking up at the financial point where
he had left off in Dublin at twenty. But within six
months he had got a number of rises and had been
promoted to manager of the department.

Presently the Edison Company was taken over by
the Bell Company and its employees formally dismissed though with an offer of re-employment in the
new concern. Had Shaw's ambition lain in telephony
(and characteristically he claimed to be the only
person in the establishment who knew its current
scientific explanation), his acquaintance with some of
the Bells in Dublin might have helped to advance him.
But he turned down the job offer and thus came to
'the end of my career as a commercial employee'.
His explanation was that he wanted to regain freedom,
but one wonders if this is the whole truth of the

matter. Might not the new job have carried less pay or lower status? For in a few months he was applying for a job with the National Telephone Company and answering other advertisements. He must have been pretty desperate at the time because he was recovering from smallpox and was obviously not able to afford to convalesce at his ease.

He had also started a second novel, *The Irrational Knot* (meaning marriage), in which he used some of his Edison experiences as a foundation for the chief character, Connolly, an Irish-American electrical engineer who, among other things, pre-echoes the young poet's farewell to Candida. Fifty years later Shaw was to introduce into *The Applecart* a not totally convincing scene in which King Magnus's platonic lady friend pulls the king to the floor in an unplatonic struggle. Shaw said the incident was based on a similar real life struggle he'd had with Mrs Pat Campbell. If so, here was yet another case of life following art, for in *The Irrational Knot* a clergyman is toppled in a struggle with an actress.

Various publishers considered *Immaturity*, rejecting it with a greater or lesser degree of reluctance. There was a marked reluctance in the case of Macmillans, whose reader is presumed to have been John Morley of the three-volume *Life of Gladstone*. The report said the reader had found 'a certain quality about it, not exactly of an attractive kind, but still not common'. Although his final verdict was that he was 'very doubtful of the expediency of publication' he was perceptive enough to record that it was 'the work of a humourist and a realist' and that 'the characters are certainly not drawn after the conventional patterns of fiction'. Chapman & Hall's reader, George Meredith, recommended rejection with one word, 'No'. But while this was in effect the same answer as Morley's the discouraging curtness strikes one as unpleasant in Meredith, reminding us that one of his earlier Noes had been directed against *Erewhon*.

In all, Shaw completed five novels in five years at the rate of five pages a day. He started a sixth (the fragment was published posthumously in an edition which is now a collector's item), but none nerved a publisher to venture capital on them. Five years after it was finished, *The Irrational Knot* began to appear as a serial in Annie Besant's magazine *Our Corner*, this being partly the result of Annie's growing personal interest in the author, partly her non-paying editor's need not to be too choosy about what she accepted to fill her pages. (For a while she paid Shaw a small fee which he accepted until he found it was coming from her private purse. He then refused to accept another penny.) Meanwhile, there had been two other significant developments in his life: he had become a convert to socialism and had developed a love life.

3

Although in later life Shaw tended to avoid the London-Irish when he could do so without causing much offence, during the first few years in London he seems to have kept up Irish acquaintanceships with no small care. One such was with James Lecky, member of a Carlow family who would have been known to him through the Gurlys, and a relation of the famous historian. Lecky, who contributed several articles to *Grove's Dictionary of Music and Musicians*, including a lucid and readable one on the tricky subject of tuning, and who included phonetics in his many interests, brought Shaw along to a meeting of a debating society called the Zetetical. It was at the Zetetical Society that, towards the end of 1879,

Shaw made his first public speech. He appeared so
self-assured that not long after he formally joined the
society he was moved to the chair for a meeting. The
secretary must have been surprised to discover the
self-assurance was merely sham. Shaw's hand shook
so much with nervousness that he could hardly sign
the minutes. He resolved to overcome this nervousness by availing himself of every opportunity to orate
in public. In due course he became one of the most
effective and sought-after public speakers of his time,
but some of those who knew him will have testified
that he never really lost his nervousness.

Lecky also introduced him to Henry Sweet, an
Oxford don with a passion for phonetics, who thirty
years later was to contribute unconsciously to the char-
acterisation of Professor Higgins in *Pygmalion*. But a
more important friendship was begun at the Zetetical
with 'an entirely unassuming young Londoner', as
Shaw in old age described him, who was 'in fact a
prodigy'. His name was Sidney Webb and Shaw 'forced'
his acquaintance on him. Webb was a little man with
a disproportionately large head and, in after years, a
Napoleon III-type goatee which suited him. They
entered each other's lives when Shaw was twenty-three
and Webb twenty. Shaw's seniority (for three years is
a significant age gap at that time of life), his genteel
background and his great advantage in height, don't
appear to have given him the least sense of superiority
to the little Cockney. In fact it was the other way
around. Shaw was profoundly impressed by Webb's
obvious natural abilities which included the power to
take in a page at a glance. (Wilde is said to have had
this power too.)

Webb's practice was not to enter into argument
until fully briefed with the facts and with all their
implications thought out. He also had the ability to
present every point clearly and cogently. Shaw was
fond of telling how when Webb was still a Colonial

Office clerk the two of them went on holiday to France. Webb brought a huge parcel of official papers to the post office and insisted that they could go through the post for a halfpenny. He told the incredulous clerk that it would be found that par. X on page X vol. X of the code entitled him to despatch official papers at this rate. The code was consulted and of course Webb was perfectly right. Shaw claimed that after this victory Webb could have posted all their laundry home for a halfpenny.

To the end of his life Shaw would sing Webb's praises extravagantly, 'the finest brain in England', 'the ablest man in England', and so on. Admiration apart, he had a deep personal fondness for Webb, although as is often the case neither admiration nor affection was returned in similar degree. However, both Sidney and Beatrice Webb fully valued Shaw's aid in their campaign to establish the socialist state, recognising how useful his gifts as a public speaker were, and how no less useful was his literary style in lightening their own rather turgid writing. A favourite quip of Shaw was that some of the most impish extravagances in his own work had been slipped in by Webb on the quiet.

Webb had an unexpected partiality for poetry and was an ardent novel reader. Shaw, whose passion for beauty of sound was adequately satisfied by music, probably had a hole where his bump of reverence for Poesy should have been. As a dramatist, accustomed to the speed of dramatic action, he found novels boring for their slow pace and tendency to linger over detailed descriptions of the wallpaper in the author's childhood bedroom and the interminable interior monologue which had to be recited before a character could bring himself to scratch his ear.

The entrance of Sidney Webb into Shaw's life more or less marked Lee's exit from it. Lee was also dis-

missed from Bessie's life. Shaw alleges two reasons.
He says that the London mammas who brought their
daughters to Lee to be taught singing were not
prepared to wait the three or four years required by
the Method to complete the training. They wanted
the girls to be turned into Pattis in ten lessons. Lee
therefore had to comply or starve. He complied,
becoming a charlatan in the process and forfeiting
Bessie's respect and regard. The second reason was
that Lee was becoming embarrassingly 'sentimental'
about Lucy, and Lucy was at an age, twenty-five
or thereabouts, at which pretty, witty girls don't
welcome the advances of elderly men they happen
to have known since early childhood and who had
a romantic entanglement with their mother. The
whole situation so disgusted Bessie that she dropped
her old mentor as ruthlessly as her father used shoot
a sporting dog on its first mistake.

There is also the possibility that Bessie had found
out how Lee was trying to pass off his Park Lane
housekeeper's daughter as the social equal of his lady
and gentleman pupils, this suggesting that the
relationship between him and the girl was closer than
one of which Bessie could approve. But although
Bessie may have excommunicated Lee, Shaw
certainly didn't, nor does Lucy appear to have
completely cut him off. They were too good-natured
for that. Besides, Lee might still be useful.

Shaw's work as Lee's musical assistant appears
to have been unpaid except perhaps by casual hospit-
ality at Park Lane and by offers of holidays. The
last of these, an invitation to join him in Scotland,
was made in August 1886, three months before
Lee's death. Writing to Shaw in January 1880, Lee
indicates that he is willing to put his hand in his
pocket: 'The enclosed is to pay for subscriptions to
liberaries and books you may require to work on

and the result that will [sic] regenerate the musical world. When more coin is wanted I shall be glad to send it.' This offer to pay out-of-pocket expenses may really be a tactful cover for a personal subvention. At any rate Shaw endorsed the note in red ink 'Retained £5'.

In August 1881 Lee wrote from Scotland:

Would it suit your proclivities at present to construct something upon whatever lines of the "Voice" etc. you might wish to adopt. Including your own observations? If so, I should like to make the action of the tongue a salient point. Its injurious influence upon the production of the voice when placed firmly and flat as in sounding A according to the Italian notion tending to [indecipherable] * rigidity of the larynx and thereby causing strain upon the internal mechanism and its absolute utility in reflecting vibration from a widely and steadily distended pharynx into the oral cavity or against the hard palate producing that travelling or penetrating quality born upon a foundation of full sound consequent upon certain positions of larynx and pharynx. It is really the mechanical consummation of voice production for public singing.

I quote at this length from the letter, partly for what it tells us about the Method, little though that may be, partly because it amply confirms what Shaw said about Lee's inability to write coherently. Lee repeats his offer 'to send you some coin as you will require it for books of reference & etc.' Shaw's draft reply, addressed from his Uncle Walter's house at Leyton and dated 24 August 1881, says he is disposed to

*Lee's surviving letters are amongst the Shaw Papers in the British Library. The handwriting is often impossible to decipher — at least I found it so.

have a shot at it, although he will not commit himself so far as to take any money. If the book came to publication stage and there were any profits, he would take a share. Lee's reply was prompt.

> I imagine that a book somewhat similar to the original "Voice" would prove most successful price either 2/6 or 5s. I could get it well noticed by Huiffer, Edwards & etc. a pamphlet would not insure such. I think I can send you a copy of the old Voice for cuttings.

Little more can have been done in the matter, for on 29 August 1883, almost exactly two years later, Lee was again writing: 'I am anxious to bring out a new edition of the "Voice" when would it suit you to give me a chat?'

But the chat, if accorded, did not lead to the completion of the enterprise. Shaw did indeed set about a new *Voice* but it was no mere revision. It was a totally different kind of book, far more readable than the original but also far less likely to impress potential singing pupils with the physiological learning of the putative author, since the approach was that of an artist using his instinct, not an anatomist brandishing drawings of our inner organs, and therefore less imposing to the layman. Whether Lee ever read what Shaw had written for him we do not know. Probably not. At any rate Shaw laid the task aside and presently Lee's death made it pointless to resume.

Little remains to be told of Lee. On 10 January 1886 Shaw noted in his diary that he had written a prospectus for Lee. A week later he called on Lee, but thereafter there is no mention of Lee in the diaries until later in the year when his death is noted. On Saturday 27 November Lee dined with some friends in a Leicester Square restaurant. After dinner he became unwell, took an omnibus home to Park

Lane and dropped dead in the act of putting an arm into the sleeve of his nightshirt. He was found the following morning. A post-mortem revealed extensive heart disease and the inquest jury returned a verdict of death from natural causes. He was fifty-five according to his death certificate but was probably a year older. The singer Hayden Coffin happened to meet Lucy on the Sunday that Lee was found dead, and told her the news. She told Shaw who went home to tell his mother. Bessie displayed no emotion.

None of the Shaws went to the funeral. They didn't even know where Lee was buried or who looked after his affairs. In fact he was buried cheaply in Woking Cemetery and his estate was administered by his landlord Julian Marshall in the role of creditor. His effects, including a balance of £135. 0s. 1d. at the St James's Square branch of the London & Westminster Bank, were valued at £602. 12s. 1d. Advertisements for the next of kin produced no response.

4

By this time Shaw's interest was centred in the Fabian Society. This had been founded in January 1884 as a group aiming to better the world by unhasty steps, a concept later memorably described by Webb as 'the inevitability of gradualness'. The society derived its title from the tactics of Fabius Cunctator, he who frustrated Hannibal's advance on Rome by strategic evasion of battle. The classical allusion suggested to Shaw that the society's members must be educated people of at least his own social standing, so he joined. The early debates are said to have been abstract and Utopian until in March 1885 Sidney Webb brought the Fabian Society down to earth with a paper called 'The Way Out'. Two months later Webb was elected a member. Within a year he [64] had joined Shaw on the executive. Two others were enrolled shortly afterwards, Sydney Olivier (a relation of Laurence) and Graham Wallas. These four were to be the mainstay of the Fabian Society all through its great period, when it was a more formidable force for change in British political life than it appeared to its contemporaries to be.

The secretary was Edward Reynolds Pease, member of a family which had made money as industrialists. This, by giving him some financial independence, enabled him to work for the society for a pound a week at the task of undermining the social structure which had permitted the family to accumulate its wealth. Which in itself provides a good example of how the Fabian Society worked. Shaw was the academically unqualified editor* of the volume of *Fabian Essays* published in 1889, his own contribution being the essays on the economic basis of socialism and on the transition to social democracy. Other contributors were Sidney Webb (LL.B, Barrister-at-Law, Lecturer on Political Economy at the City of London College); William Clarke (M.A., Cambridge); Sydney Olivier (B.A., Oxford); Graham Wallas (M.A., Oxford). Two other contributors, Annie Besant and Hubert Bland, were, like Shaw, officially uneducated. *Fabian Essays* had an unexpected success.

The enlargement of his circle of friends and acquaintances brought about by his participation in Lee's musical activities and in those of the Fabian Society had an inevitable outcome. This was the first flowering of a long series of emotional relationships with women.

*Or rather 'the nominal editor' as he said in the unsigned short preface, merely the person 'told off to arrange for the publication of the papers, and see them through the press with whatever editorial ceremony might be necessary'.

In his Dublin days he had few opportunities to get [65] acquainted with girls. Although he had two sisters their departure when he was seventeen deprived him of the chance to meet their friends and their friends' friends, and, as we have seen, few invitations to family parties came his way. Since young ladies did not go out to work in those days the land agent's office was another sex Sahara for him, and his fellow-lodgers in the Harcourt Street house were bachelors. A less shy and inhibited youth would have found a way to overcome these impediments, or would have purchased sex on the street. But apart from an old Dublin legend that he had been much smitten by a darkhaired local beauty named Marie Campbell, we have no hint of any big romance before he boarded the mailboat in 1876. This does not surprise us. But what astounds us to the point of incredulity is his claim that not only did he remain a virgin for the nine years of his semi-bohemian life in London but that he was perfectly continent 'except for the involuntary incontinences of dreamland'. Catholic priests are supposed to be able to achieve this way of love-life with the aid of sanctifying grace and under the compulsions of a vow of chastity. What is difficult to understand is how Shaw managed to do it without these reinforcements, except on the assumption that he was impotent (which he denied with dignity) or undersexed (which he denied vehemently).

His loss of virginity was a direct result of his father's death. GCS had ended up as a lodger in No. 21 Leeson Park Avenue, a smallish house in a cul de sac not far away from his partner Clibborn's residence. There, on 19 April 1885, in his seventy-second year, he died from 'congestion of the lungs'. Neither Shaw nor his mother returned to Dublin for the funeral. Almost certainly they hadn't the ready money for the journey, and may also have feared that by presenting themselves as chief mourners they might be made responsible for the funeral expenses (probably between £10 and £12). Lucy is supposed to have been in Dublin at the time of her father's death and to have been on affectionate terms with him, but did not attend the funeral to Mount Jerome. She has been criticised for this, it not being realised that it was then the custom for ladies not to join the cortege to the cemetery.

His brother Frederick attended to the necessary arrangements and in due course notified Bessie that she would be receiving about £100, the proceeds of an insurance policy on GCS's life. Bessie gave part of the money to Shaw to fit himself out with new clothes, he having become dreadfully shabby. His diary tells us what the purchases were. An all-wool suit made by Jaegers (£5.15s.), black coat and vest (£4. 4s.), collars (4s.), cravat (2s.), pants (16s.), a total of just over £11. He alleged that his sudden appearance in presentable garments propelled dazzled women into his arms, one of them succeeding, in the early hours of his twenty-ninth birthday, in taking the citadel. The enterprising lady was Mrs Jenny Patterson, a singing pupil of his mother. Jenny had been on friendly terms with Bessie and Lucy since at least 1878. She was a widow who admitted to being forty-four, although if the age stated on her death certificate is correct she would have been only forty-one in 1885. Shaw himself, however, is quoted as saying that she told him the difference in their ages was fifteen years.

Like almost all the women Shaw got himself involved with at this stage of his life, Jenny Patterson was large and fleshy. And like the other women she also had money. Some biographers suspect that Jenny wished to marry Shaw and that his mother and sister hoped she would. There is no firm evidence as to Jenny's intentions, but the jealousy and possessiveness she displayed later on, culminating in an attempted physical attack on a rival, suggest that she might not have turned down a proposal had Shaw made one. He is believed to have sent a detailed account of his seduction to Matt McNulty but of course this no longer exists. Shaw's diary, however, tersely records the salient facts. For some weeks he had been calling to Jenny's home quite late in the evening. As far back as April he had left a concert conducted by Richter in order to visit her and stayed until midnight. In July he was with her until one a.m. Later that month the diary mentions 'Supper, music and curious conversation, and a declaration of passion' without making it clear from which side the declaration came. On 25 July he called on Jenny in the afternoon and found his mother there. He left, returning at 11.00 p.m. to find his mother still there. He escorted her to a bus and returned to Jenny's, staying until 3.00 a.m. and celebrating the dawn of his birthday 'by a new experience'.

In his year's end summary he noted in the diary, 'I was an absolute novice. I did not take the initiative in the matter.'

Although Jenny was, so to speak, first past the post she did not monopolise him, or rather she could not. Earlier his interest had been aroused by another of his mother's pupils, a nurse named Alice Lockett, whom he upset by some kind of love declaration when escorting her to a railway station. Nearly a dozen of his love letters to her have survived and these, like his other love letters, betray the struggle between a natural impulse to mate and a temperamental need to remain free of personal ties. A passage in the letter implies that he and Alice were on kissing terms but their relationship appears not to have gone

any further than that. Alice married a doctor,
Salisbury Sharpe, and for several years was to keep
her nurse's eye on Shaw and get her husband to
attend to him when necessary.

Simultaneously Shaw was becoming involved with
his fellow-Fabian Mrs Annie Besant, estranged wife of
a clergyman, a highly effective public speaker and an
earnest fighter for women's rights. Annie Besant (née
Wood) was related to Kitty O'Shea (née Wood),
which established a link between Parnell and Shaw.
(If Shaw was aware of this he never mentioned it.)
How far things went with Annie we don't know, but
presently she drew up the terms upon which she
proposed to live with him in a free association, her
notion of a free association being dismissed by him as
worse than any marriage contract. The wife of
another Fabian colleague, Hubert Bland, also took a
fancy to him. Mrs Bland, well known in her day for
her children's stories published under the name
Edith Nesbit, would probably have been glad to
submit to any adulterous demands he made. But
Shaw was punctilious about refraining from any
action which might endanger another man's marriage,
even though the other man might be endangering it
himself, as Bland was doing, with a reckless series of
affairs. Besides, Bland was a practised pugilist and not
at all scrupulous about using his fists on non-
combatant types who had offended him. The
relationship with Mrs Bland remained within the
limits of propriety as understood by the Fabians, for
these limits were broader than those set by suburbia
at that time. She used to require him to accompany
her on late evening walks, sometimes releasing him
only after his last train had left. Otherwise she went
no further than to address verses to him, which were
published. Although he wasn't named there were
certain indications as to his identity which were

unlikely to have escaped the brethren. Mrs Bland, wearing her prose hat, pronounced him plain. Under her poet's hat she found his white face 'maddening', and his cleverness and humour additionally attractive.

It has to be conceded that at this period the famous face was not entirely prepossessing. Its pallor was disturbed by a reddish nose and by a mop of plastered down orange red (some said auburn) hair, his cheeks being fringed with the fluffy beginnings of a ginger whisker. The beard was such a slow developer that most men would have shaved it away through shame. But Shaw let nature take her leisurely course and the beard's ultimate luxuriance must be accounted yet another vindication of its owner's inner faith in his powers. Meanwhile the countenance, later so impressive, was likened by a Fabian colleague to an imperfectly poached egg.

Not that this drove the women away. There was the artist Bertha Newcome who made a flattering portrait of him as an exuberant orator and who felt that he owed her marriage. There was another girl who seemed ripe for romance but was saved by the vigorous intervention of her aunt who sent Shaw packing unceremoniously, indeed humiliatingly. There was Henry Salt's wife — a wife only in name, though, for she was lesbian — who gave Shaw good reason to claim that she loved him as much as she was capable of loving any man. And there was May Morris.

May Morris was daughter of William, a man so various that the litany of his accomplishments makes him sound something of a jack-of-all-trades. He was poet, craftsman, designer, interior decorator, printer, lecturer, Utopian novelist and founder of the Socialist League. May Morris was reputed to be arrestingly beautiful. The reputation may have been well founded but her photographs don't bear this out. One which was taken of her when she was still a young woman makes her look like Sir Henry Irving's older brother in drag. Morris became interested enough in Shaw, partly because of the novel serialised in Annie Besant's magazine, partly through hearing some of his lectures on socialism, to admit him to his circle of friends and to have him to dinner at his artistically furnished house in Hammersmith. It was here that Shaw met May and was yet again smitten. In his dramatisation of their relationship he has May coming from the dining room into the hall one Sunday evening as he was leaving after supper. Her lovely dress and lovely self must have brought an unmistake-able glint into his eye, and he alleges that she responded by carefully and deliberately making 'a gesture of assent' with *her* eye. He interpreted this as a 'Mystical Betrothal' which had been straightaway registered in Heaven, bidding them both to marriage when he was in a position to support a wife. Mean-while the betrothal was not to interfere with his other affairs.

The account of the Mystical Betrothal, which it would be an unfriendly act to quote in full, so reminiscent is it of the style of Barbara Cartland, was given in his contribution to a volume about Morris edited by May and published in 1936. On first reading his contribution May exclaimed, 'Really, Shaw!' But she decided to publish and be saved, for its tributes to her past loveliness were irresistibly flattering to a woman of seventy-four with a distinct moustache. Besides, Shaw was at the height of his celebrity and any volume with something by him in it sold well.

But to return to the Hammersmith of the 1880s. If May was aware of any Mystical Betrothal it did not prevent her from claiming the same freedom in her relationship with men as Shaw claimed for himself with women. Presently she married Halliday

Sparling, the law of the attraction of opposites having once more asserted itself. Anything less like a fitting mate for the stately May Morris it would be hard to imagine. St John Ervine with Ulster brutality likened him to Uriah Heep's grandson. The marriage was an astonishing move on May's part, Sparling being as poor as Shaw and, to all appearances at that time, just as futureless. She may have really fallen for the little frail looking man, instinctively feeling that she herself had enough stature and muscle for two, or for the reason given by one of Shaw's characters for some women's decision to take a husband. In *Fanny's First Play*, Juggins says, 'Women don't always marry for happiness, sir. They often marry because they wish to be married women and not old maids.'

An interesting development followed May's marriage to little Sparling, who seems to have been as unassertive a husband as George Carr Shaw. Shaw did a Vandeleur Lee on them, moving into their home and establishing a *mènage à trois* resembling the Hatch Street one, although the parallel seems never to have struck him. What role May played in this move is a matter for speculation. Obviously she would have to be willing, and it is likely that she would have put up some proposals, however vague, as to what Shaw's standing should be in the house, whether as friend coming for an indefinite stay, or as a lodger. The results in the Sparling household were not dissimilar to those in Hatch Street. The hostess's initial special attention to the guest appears to have increased rather than diminished as time went on, tensions built up and Shaw says that when he saw what he was doing to his host's marriage he packed his bags and left. Whether or not his cuckoo incursion had caused the problem or merely exacerbated an existing one, his departure did not solve it. The marriage broke up, May resuming her single life and maiden name.

But all this does not complete the Don Giovanni
list of Shaw's lady friends at this time. Earlier he had
started an affair with Florence Farr, estranged wife of
an actor named Emery, an affair in which pleasure
was combined with business. The business probably
ranked as the more important aspect to Shaw, for
the conclusion is inescapable that although in his
head he was an ardent and scrupulous feminist, in his
heart he regarded women as sex objects who also
came in handy for secretarial and other services and
had a special usefulness in the theatre as actresses. In
April 1894 it was Florence who gave *Arms and the Man*
its first production; it was also Shaw's first real introduction to the West End as a playwright and therefore his first step to commercial success. For Shaw
had now at long last turned playwright, thanks to
the entrance into his life of another important friend,
William Archer.

6

William Archer was two months younger than Shaw.
He was born in Perth on 23 September 1856. The
Archers, like many other Scottish families, had
business and family connections with Scandinavia.
Much of William's childhood was spent at his grandfather Archer's home in Larvik in Norway. Norwegian
became a second language to him, and might easily
have become his first. His father, the nomadic type,
travelled the world, practising a variety of occupations
from sheep farming in Australia to fighting Indians
and prospecting for gold in California. As he brought
his family around with him, William Archer at twenty-
nine was exceptionally widely travelled and something
of a linguist. Nonetheless William managed to get a
conventional education, graduating at Edinburgh, and
after a false start in law turned to London journalism.

Archer was a journalist with a difference. He was no Grub-Streeter by temperament, but fortunately for him there were plenty of journals and magazines in existence of the type now known as 'quality,' in which he was able to place enough of his work to be, compared with Shaw at the same period, quite well off. He soon built up a reputation as a specialist in art matters. In Larvik one day he had overheard a lady remark that Ibsen's *Love's Comedy* was brilliantly witty. Feeling that if there was anything brilliantly witty in Norwegian he should read it, he did so, going on from that to read everything of Henrik Ibsen he could lay hands on. He ended up a disciple, resolved to spread the gospel of St Henrik in Britain. (The canonisation was Shaw's doing.)

How Shaw and Archer first met is something neither could remember. Shaw left his readers with the impression that the event occurred in the reading room of the British Museum, as it might well have done. He added a few dramatic touches to his own part in the scene, having himself seated before copies of *Das Kapital* and a Wagner score, Archer being cast in the supporting role of fascinated spectator. At any rate their first encounter was in 1885 and acquaintance soon developed into affectionate friendship, with Archer determined to help Shaw to get openings in journalism. This he succeeded in doing, procuring book reviewing for him in the *Pall Mall Gazette* and art reviewing in *The World*. Getting Shaw to avail himself of these opportunities was hard work: he had to be continually pushed into accepting commissions, for his real interest was centred in the Fabian Society and the improvement of the world's condition rather than his own. But thanks to William Archer and to Jenny Patterson he ended the year 1885 with an earned income from journalism of £117 and the right to call himself an experienced man.

Archer had published a book called *English Drama-*
[74] *tists of Today*. It didn't cause publishers to beat a
track to his door but it did get him the post of
dramatic critic of *The World* at three guineas (£3.15)
a week. As critic he had, beside a first-hand knowledge of Ibsen, another useful advantage over rivals.
Having in childhood been obliged to listen to chunks
of the Bible being read out to him, he trained himself
to sleep while sitting bolt upright with his eyes wide
open. By exercising this faculty he could sit through
West End plays night after night without damaging
his health. He also developed the conviction, rare
enough in civilised communities although quite
common amongst the Irish, that there's nothing to
writing a play. If you accepted the old teaching that
mankind has so far managed to invent only nine
plots (of which no more than two are used in modern
television drama), then the sensible procedure was
to lift a plot from the nearest French play and add
dialogue to taste. The trouble was that while Archer
was convinced of his ability to lift plots he fell back
in defeat before the task of providing the dialogue.

A brilliant solution presented itself. He would give
Shaw the plot, Shaw would run off the dialogue
and, by repeating the process ad lib., their fortunes
would be made. Shaw was enthusiastic, declaring that
he was hopeless with plots but a wizard at dialogue.
He set to work and shortly afterwards came back to
Archer for more plot, alleging that the original
supply had all been used up in a few pages of dialogue.
This is so obviously a Shavianisation of the episode
that we must not take it literally. But the result was
the shelving of the play, either because Archer with-
drew from so impossible a collaboration or because
Shaw lost interest.

Archer had however communicated his Ibsen
enthusiasm to Shaw, who promptly bettered his

instruction by proclaiming Ibsen greater than Shakespeare at many points, which naturally irrit- ated Archer. Shaw increased this irritation by paying less regard to Ibsen the lyric poet, the side which most attracted Archer, than to Ibsen the prophet and reformer of morals, the side which naturally attracted himself and didn't particularly appeal to Archer. Shaw virtually took over Ibsen from Archer, in the summer of 1890 delivering a substantial lecture on the dramatist to the Fabians. The lecture was later developed into a treatise which, as *The Quintessence of Ibsenism*, is still without rival as an exposition of the subject and one of the brightest masterpieces of literary criticism of our era.

Meanwhile the cast of the Shaw drama had been joined by another Irishman, Thomas Power ('Tay-Pay') O'Connor.

7

O'Connor, who was not quite the nincompoop Shaw implied he was, was born in Athlone in 1848 and thus was Shaw's senior by eight years. His family could not afford to make him the barrister he aspired to be, so he turned to journalism as a junior reporter on an old Dublin paper *Saunders Newsletter*, which had been founded in the eighteenth century and never left it. In 1870 O'Connor went to London for a holiday, with £4 in his pocket. The silhouette of the Houses of Parliament against the evening sky inspired him to stay in London to become a states-man and a great author. He walked into the office of the *Daily Telegraph* and was straightaway offered a job at £3 a week, more than three times what he had been getting in Dublin. His luck held. In 1876, the year Shaw arrived in London, O'Connor publish-ed a biography of Disraeli which was so effectively critical of the great Tory champion, that O'Connor became a darling of the Liberals. At thirty he was elected MP for Galway in the Home Rule interest, became a prominent member of Parnell's party and, when the Liberals decided to publish an evening paper, was appointed editor and managing director at a salary of £1,200 a year plus a share of the profits.

The Star was started on £40,000 subscribed by Henry Labouchere and other rich Liberals, and like every newspaper that ever was or ever well be, declared that it would be progressive. Accordingly Tay-Pay and his lieutenants recruited a team of young contributors with reputations as Progressives but with sufficient moral flexibility to be able to subordinate Progress to Prudence when writing for *The Star*. Among these was Sidney Webb, concerning which high-priest of socialism Tay-Pay knew so little that he begged him 'not to antagonize the socialists'. Other recruits to *The Star* included Henry Hyndman and Arthur Bingham Walkley, later eminent as drama critic of *The Times* and immortalised as the dedicatee of *Man and Superman*, greatest of Shaw's comedies. Shaw was also taken on as a staff writer.

Now *The Star* was better named than O'Connor realised. A star gives little light and no heat, which was just the way Tay-Pay wanted things to be. Shaw wasn't long upsetting this. After a few issues the paper's financial backers descended upon Tay-Pay to enquire what the devil he meant by playing socialist tunes on a Liberal organ. The result was the suppression of Shaw's articles. Finding himself in much the same situation as he had been in Townshend's office after being superseded as cashier, he resigned. Tay-Pay later claimed that since he 'could not think of putting a man back into the abyss [of unemployment] from which he had only just emerged,' he had accordingly allowed Shaw to be kept on as music critic. But although Tay-Pay's good nature was genuine enough, he did in fact allow Shaw to be hurled back into the abyss, leaving him to scrape along for the next year on a slender revenue from occasional articles and as a stand-in for *The Star*'s regular music critic, Ernest Belfort Bax, uncle of the composer Arnold Bax and of the writer Clifford Bax. It was not until February 1889, a year after his resignation, that Shaw replaced Bax as official critic. Bax had written under the pseudonym Musigena. Shaw became Corno di Bassetto (the Italian for basset horn) and soon was probably the most eagerly read and talked about music critic in London.

That Corno di Bassetto was always amusing and perceptive goes without saying. That he was sometimes wrong, and disastrously so, now matters little, although it may have mattered a great deal at the time except when his targets were, like Brahms and Dvorak, too firmly established to be affected by anything he wrote, good or bad. But certain misapprehensions, later fostered by himself, have grown up about his criticisms: for instance, that he was a lone fighter for the cause of Wagner in London. This is nonsense. Wagner was so well thought of in London, even by that hotbed of conservatism the Royal Philharmonic Society, that he had been invited to conduct some of its concerts in 1855 and again in 1877, Shaw being at this concert. His operas had first been performed in London long before Shaw started writing on music, and in the case of *The Flying Dutchman* and *Lohengrin* before he had even arrived in London. *The Flying Dutchman* was performed there in 1870; *Lohengrin* 1875; *Tannhauser* 1876; *Tristan, The Mastersingers* and the complete *Ring* in 1882.

An anthology can be compiled from Shaw's music criticisms both as 'Corno di Bassetto' and as the maturer and more penetrating GBS who was critic of *The World* from 1890 to 1894, which, read out of context, would show him to have been wrongheaded, ignorant, narrowminded, uncomprehending and even malicious. A critic who cried up Gounod's *Faust* and cried down Schubert's Great C major Symphony, declaring the now venerated finale to be hardly up to the level of a Rossini overture, would appear to have put himself out of court. But in their context, Shaw's pronouncements seem less eccentric, less bizarre than when viewed in isolation. The criticisms, taken as a whole, constitute a kind of Candid Confessions of a Musical Man, forming a self-portrait, warts and all, that become acceptable as a record of immediate reactions honestly set down. His writings on music, gathered into four volumes in his own lifetime, were re-issued in 1981 in another edition prepared with awesome conscientiousness by Dan H. Laurence. They remain our most readable musical journalism, because for most of the time Shaw was setting down his reactions to what he actually heard, not what he was supposed to hear, putting small value on reputations and academic qualifications if he thought the music did not live up to them.

Inevitably there were self-deceptions, delusions and prejudices, such as everyone suffers. For instance, Dvorak was trounced merely for being a Bohemian by birth. Then there was the already mentioned delusion that he was playing St John the Baptist to Wagner's Redeemer, this producing the silly anti-Brahmsism which one would expect so acute and vigilant a critic to have carefully steered himself clear of. Again one wonders what he can have heard in Goetz's rather pedestrian Symphony in F that inspired him to hail it as a masterpiece which, with his opera *The Taming of the Shrew*, placed Goetz above all other German composers of the previous hundred years save only Mozart and Beethoven, Weber and Wagner. Thus Haydn and Schubert, Schumann, Mendelssohn and Brahms were left out in the cold by this judgment. Yet when all is said and done, one has only to glance at the work of the other London critics of that era to see how Corno di Bassetto and GBS of *The World* outshone them at most points, bequeathing to us the most vivid word picture of a half-decade of music-making we are every likely to have.

And both *The Star* and *The World* got all this treasure on the cheap: the former for two guineas a week, the latter for five pounds.

During his period as *The World*'s music critic Shaw had been edging closer and closer to the theatre, still apparently not realising that it was there his true kingdom lay. His enthusiasm for Ibsen was maintained. In 1891 he got his actress girlfriend Florence Farr to produce *Rosmersholm* with herself as Rebecca West. Florence, who had by now displaced Jenny Patterson in his love life, provided him with what he delicately hinted were sex adventures of the Frank Harris kind, so we can surmise that their affair was, by the Shavian scale of romance, quite torrid. Florence was a daughter of William Farr (1807-83), a medical doctor and a statistician who entered the registrar-general's office and became superintendent of the statistics department. He was the author of *Vital Statistics* (published posthumously) and although he appears to have outlived his wits and to have lost much of his savings in foolish speculations at the end, he still left enough to give Florence a certain independence, thus qualifying her financially for the role of Shaw's companion.

A few weeks after Florence had produced *Rosmersholm* J. T. Grein produced Ibsen's *Ghosts* at his newly founded Independent Theatre. This highly moral play caused the London critics to surpass themselves in idiocy, creating a record for bad-tempered obtuseness which remained unbroken until the Dublin critics set about O'Casey's *The Bishop's Bonfire*. In his introduction to *The Quintessence of Ibsenism* Shaw quoted with relish a selection of their comments. *The Daily Telegraph* declared that Ibsen had taken ideas that would have inspired a great tragic poet and used them to produce loathsome, horrible plays. For good measure the paper added in a leading article that *Ghosts* was an open drain, a loathsome sore unbandaged, a dirty act done publicly, a lazar house with all its doors and windows open. *The Standard*, the leading Tory paper, wanted proceedings taken against the theatre management under the act for the suppression of disorderly houses. And so on.

Needless to say this was just what was needed to establish the Independent Theatre with progressives as the latest fashionable venue for shock therapy. Grein, a Dutch Jew connected with the tea trade, angled for a play from Shaw. This caused Shaw to take down again the unfinished play he had started with Archer. He hurriedly provided a third act and the play, entitled *Widowers' Houses*, was produced at the Royalty Theatre on 9 December 1892. A matinee was given on the 13th.

The play, which deals with slum landlordism and the way its profits contaminate so-called 'independent' incomes, clearly draws on the activities of the author's pawnbroking great-grandfather whose profits, in the form of the Whitcroft legacy, had helped to keep Shaw alive in the early London days, and on his own experiences in the land agent's office. Although *Widowers' Houses* received only two performances at the time, the reputation earned for the Independent Theatre by *Ghosts* and the author's own reputation with his journalist colleagues got the play discussed for a week in the daily papers and attracted two leading articles. The critics, not knowing that most of the play had been written before Shaw had really got to know his Ibsen, shook their sapient heads over the baleful Norwegian influence it exhibited.

The author's good friend Florence Farr played the part of Blanche Sartorius, the hot tempered bullying heroine, a character based on Jenny Patterson. Jenny herself, and Shaw's mother, were in the audience but apparently neither spotted any resemblances.

Shaw continued his portraiture of friends and acquaintances in his next play, *The Philanderer*, which followed hard on the heels of *Widowers' Houses*. The ineffable Clement Scott, the critic of *The Daily Telegraph* who had been so conspicuous a victim of Ibsen-shock, is the silly but likeable Joe Cuthbertson, a critic in the play as in life. *The Philanderer* has in general had a bad press. Even St John Ervine, for all his veneration of Shaw, dismisses it as 'singularly lacking in vivacity and wit'. He may have taken his cue from Shaw himself who in a letter to Ellen Terry savaged *The Philanderer* as 'a combination of mechanical farce with realistic filth which quite disgusted me'. But anyone who reads or sees *The Philanderer* would be hard put to it, as Ervine himself was, to find any trace of 'realistic filth'. A possible explanation is that Shaw, when writing to Ellen Terry, was in full reaction against that period of his life when his involvement with several women at the same time caused outbursts of female jealousy in which he literally had to pull Jenny Patterson off Florence Farr. Indeed it is the Jenny-Florence tussle over himself which is the mainspring of the play, the character of the philanderer

Leonard Charteris being an easily recognisable self-portrait. But while *The Philanderer* is unquestionably one of Shaw's lesser plays, it is far from being the dull affair that Ervine and its other critics imply it is. When it was revived in 1982 by Phyllis Ryan in Dublin's Gate Theatre, with a brilliant impersonation of Shaw-Charteris by Alan Stanford, it kept the audience laughing their heads off and achieved a seven-weeks' run, a lengthy one by Dublin standards for 'legit' drama nowadays.

The Philanderer did not achieve its first performance until 1907, fourteen years after its composition, when it was given a run of eight matinees at the Royal Court Theatre in London. Joe Cuthbertson was played by Luigi Lablache, son of the well-known singer who had often appeared in Dublin, his mother having been guest star at Lee's Exhibition concerts. Criticism of *The Philanderer* is justified in as much as it did not mark the kind of advance on its predecessor that, say, Beethoven achieved with his Second Symphony. But, if one may risk taking this rather hazardous analogy one step further, Shaw's next play, *Mrs Warren's Profession*, is his Eroica: the first unmistakeable masterwork of a major dramatist. Like the symphony, it impresses the audience with its strength and unwavering assurance.

Its thesis is that prostitution is not caused by male lust or female depravity but by so underpaying women who have to work for a living that they are forced to sell themselves to remain alive. In this play, as in most Shaw plays, the women are the superiors of the men. Even Mrs Warren, managing director of a chain of continental hotel-brothels, seems a more acceptable kind of person than her fellow-director and former lover Sir George Crofts. The most striking character, however, is Mrs Warren's daughter Vivie, a dramatisation of that constantly recurring phenomenon the New Woman. Here again Shaw has been drawing from the life, for Vivie sounds remarkably like Beatrice Webb, with touches of Florence Farr. Florence would probably have played the part were it not that the play was refused a licence by the Lord Chamberlain, to Shaw's fury. This meant it could be presented to the public only in printed form, or in private performances at a theatre club. *Mrs Warren's Profession*, dealing as it does in a serious, unsensational style with prostitution as an industry, and with incest as what musicians would call a 'second subject', was obviously not destined for box-office success. The Lord Chamberlain's asinine ban gave Shaw ammunition for his long anti-censorship campaign. He pointed out again and again that if he had treated prostitution in the vein of farce or romance, with the prostitutes all young, pretty, disease-free and with hearts of gold, or if he had regarded venereal disease as a transient and amusing inconvenience as the Restoration dramatists did, then the play would have been licensed as readily as other such plays were by the simpleminded Chamberlain. (The Lord Chamberlain did not personally deal with plays submitted for licensing. He appointed an Official Reader to do the job and pocketed the two guinea fee. Shaw strenuously objected to having to pay two guineas for permission to stage a play.) As things stood, Shaw could only have *Mrs Warren's Profession* put on in London by a theatre club, the Stage Society, whose performances, being technically private, did not fall under official displeasure. Three years after the Stage Society performance (1902) the play was produced in America, creating a sensation which culminated in the arrest of the producer. (The judge threw out the case.) The play was a success in Germany, helping to spread Shaw's reputation there, of which he was always

proud; it was also a success in Paris (1912) although
without any lasting effect on the author's reputation
there. It was not until 1925 that *Mrs Warren's
Profession*, then thirty-two years old (and its author
sixty-nine), received its first performance in London's
West End.

8

Florence Farr's excursions into actor-managership
drew the attention of Annie E. F. Horniman (1860-
1937), who had some claims to be in the New Woman
line herself. Like J. T. Grein she was connected with
the tea trade, being a member of a family made rich
by that beverage. The family had a Puritan attitude
to drama, or at any rate to the theatre, regarding it
as a gate to hell. Miss Horniman accordingly had to
keep her theatrical patronage a nervously kept secret.
She was also the benefactor of the Gaiety Theatre in
Manchester and of the Abbey Theatre in Dublin. In
financing a short season for Florence Farr at the
Avenue Theatre in Northumberland Avenue, Miss
Horniman enjoined her not to mention this to a soul.
The Avenue Theatre season was virtually an Irish
season. Miss Horniman probably suggested that Yeats's
Land of Heart's Desire be included, for she was a
friend of Yeats and may have been in love with him.
The second play was *The Comedy of Sighs* by that
other figure from the Dublin past, Dr John Todhunter.
Neither piece captivated the public, the dismal
failure of Todhunter's play causing Florence to turn in
desperation to Shaw for permission to revive *Widowers'
Houses*. He for his part, preferring to provide a new
play rather than have an unsatisfactory one revived,
hurriedly finished *Arms and the Man*. (First called
Alps and Balkans, an obvious crib from Samuel Butler's
Alps and Sanctuaries, published in 1881.) It was

hurriedly put into rehearsal and received a first performance described by St John Ervine as 'boisterous'.

This was the performance at which one of Shaw's most famous repartees was delivered. As he took his curtain call and the enthusiastic applause stopped for the author's speech, a hiss came from someone in the gallery. Shaw bowed and said, 'I quite agree with you sir, but what can two do against so many?' The someone was Reginald Golding Bright (1874-1941), later a successful literary agent but at that time a clerk who aspired to dramatic criticism. Rather oddly, he wrote to the author he had just hissed asking advice on how to become a drama critic. Shaw, presumably not knowing it was Golding Bright who had hissed him, sent him one of his usual full, civil and sensible replies, and the correspondence continued intermittently for some years.

Arms and the Man received enough praise from the critics to gratify Florence Farr and console Miss Horniman for the failure of the season as a whole. It grossed £1,777 but unfortunately only at the average rate of £22 2s. 5d. per night of its eleven weeks run. This made it a financial failure. Nevertheless it confirmed Shaw in his resolution to conquer the stage, incidentally bringing him £90 in royalties.

At this point it is proper to remind the reader that although the unfinished *Widowers' Houses* had been completed and *The Philanderer, Mrs Warren's Profession*, and *Arms and the Man* all written in a relatively short period, Shaw was not a full-time playwright. He was turning out a substantial column of music criticism every week, as well as book reviews and articles on widely varied subjects; his voluminous correspondence would in itself constitute the whole day's labour of many a writer; he was philandering almost as much as ever; and was expending himself recklessly as a lecturer and public speaker on Fabian socialism and a dozen other themes from vegetarianism to pornography. He had become a vegetarian at about twenty-five years of age, being already a teetotaller and a non-smoker. Besides, in 1897 he delightedly allowed himself to be returned unopposed as a vestryman of St Pancras, a London borough. (Some harmless jobbery was involved: another candidate was to be let in unopposed elsewhere.) With joy he threw himself into the discussion of drains, dustbins and municipal gas. Far from his vestry work proving the last straw it seemed to have a tonic effect on him, setting him thinking of a political career, for not even he could escape the Irish national weakness for politics and/or religion.

By this time he had ceased to be music critic for *The World* and was the *Saturday Review*'s drama critic. In May 1894 the death of *The World*'s editor, Edmund Yates, had robbed Shaw of the only kind of editor he was prepared to work for: a man not afraid of his own shadow and willing to give contributors a free hand this side of libel. The new editor did not seem such a man. Shaw resigned, but at the new editor's request stayed on for a while to prevent people interpreting his departure from *The World* as a vote of no confidence. He was not to remain at a loose end for long. Frank Harris, who had just acquired *The Saturday Review*, offered him the post of drama critic at £6 a week, an advance of £1 on *The World*. He accepted, thus entering for better or for worse into lifelong enslavement to the Theatre Devil and all his works and pomps.

There must have been times too when he felt he had entered into life enslavement to Frank Harris and all *his* works and pomps. One of the comicalities of the Shaw-Harris saga is that for many years neither knew that the other had been born in Ireland, and at about the same time. Even after twenty years of fairly close acquaintanceship (one can hardly use the term friendship) Harris was under the impression that Shaw was a Yorkshireman, an impression probably deriving from one of Shaw's throwaway remarks: that he was a typical Irishman, his family had come from Hampshire. Whether Shaw knew or cared where Harris came from is open to question, although there's a touch of irony in Henry Higgins's creator not being able to spot that Harris had been born and bred in Ireland, even if the Harrisian accent was influenced by Welsh parentage and worldwide travels. Frank Harris, born in Galway in 1855, had brains above his station and therefore almost inevitably became a member of the chequered-career class. He claimed to have been labourer, cowboy, and member of the Kansas Bar, before becoming, at the age of twenty-nine, editor of the London *Evening News*. He married a rich widow, nearly twenty years older than himself, and with her money became a resident of Park Lane who hobnobbed with Lord Randolph Churchill and the future King Edward VII. His free and easy ways with his wife's money, and with a succession of younger women, caused the rich widow to detach herself from Harris, though without divorcing him, thereby throwing him back to live on his wits.

At this period of his life Frank Harris appeared able to do this well enough. For the *Saturday Review* he acquired a first-rate team: H. G. Wells, Arnold Bennett, D. S. McColl. Harris had the makings of an excellent editor if only he could be got to put his mind to the work. But he never succeeded in retaining the modest amount of active interest in the several magazines he edited to keep them in health and in his possession. He was forced either to sell them or to abandon them, and by the time he really began to feel and to fear the pinch of poverty he was a spent force. He was reputed to be a black-mailer, using 'investigative journalism' to make the victims buy him off, and manipulating his financial articles to boost certain shares with a view to profit-able dealings. He will reappear in these pages, but for the present must figure merely as Shaw's editor in the 1895-8 stint as dramatic critic.

During these years Shaw's reputation as a journal-ist grew considerably, partly because in those days the theatre was more popular than the concert hall and accordingly there were more readers of the theatre column in their paper than of the music column. Besides he was by now a matured critic and an accomplished literary craftsman. His biting critic-isms of Shakespeare scandalised many, including his venerated Samuel Butler who in his *Notebooks* said:

> I have long been repelled by this man though at the same time attracted by his coruscating power . . . His cult of Ibsen disgusts me . . . Of course Bunyan is better than Shakespeare in some respects, so is Bernard Shaw himself, so am I, so is everybody . . . but I cannot forgive Bernard Shaw for sneering at Shakespeare . . . If he means it, there is no trusting his judgment — if he does not mean it I have no time to waste on such trifling.

Shaw believed that the only way to really impress the public with your point of view is to overstate it with apparent recklessness. Sometimes he went over the top:

> With the single exception of Homer, there is no eminent writer, not even Sir Walter Scott, whom I can despise so entirely as I despise Shakespeare when I measure my mind against his.

He maintained that the irritation provoked by such

comments merely proved the need for making them, Bardolatry (as he called it) having been carried to [89] preposterous lengths. What made him formidable as a critic of Shakespeare was that he wrote from intimate knowledge of the plays, at least a dozen of which he obviously knew inside out. He also wrote from real affection for the Bard. But if he began with a measurement of mind against mind, he ended with a measurement of his work against Shakespeare's, declaring that he was either nothing or the recognised peer of Shakespeare and Moliere. Many would grant him parity with Moliere, but would draw back from placing him beside Shakespeare, though they would be ready enough to accord him second place in the hierarchy. A case, perhaps, of Shaw being Primate of English Drama and Shakespeare Primate of All English Drama.

Apart from his snappings at Shakespeare's heels, it is hard to recall any instance where he failed to recognise real merit either in plays or in players, or repeated the kind of misjudgment he often perpetrated as music critic. His lofty dismissal of *The Importance of Being Earnest* can be cited against him, but although there is something to be said for his view of it as a 'heartless' play, and although he could have faulted the absence of sharp definition in the characters of the two young couples, still it is wiser for his admirers to concede that his treatment of *The Importance* was the exception that proved the rule in his criticisms. Again he may have been more cordial towards men like Henry Arthur Jones than posterity has been. But all in all few critics in any discipline have been able to write so vigorously, so interestingly and so wittily as he did, with so few of their judgments being reversed by the appeal court of a later age.

4
Marriage

1

Shaw entered his forties in poor health. He had been overworking for twenty years and Bessie's indifference to housekeeping, not to mention the chronic lack of money, had left him seriously undernourished. It is virtually certain that he wouldn't have seen forty-five had it not been for Charlotte Payne-Townshend.

The sudden death of Charlotte's father in 1885 was a double affliction to her in that it was her adored father who had gone and her hated mother who remained. She lost little time in asserting her independence. In her case this was not just an attitude of mind but a financial reality, Horatio Payne-Townshend having left his daughters enough money to provide each with £4,000 a year. Charlotte's sister Cissy had gladdened her mother's heart by marrying a well-connected horsey colonel from Shropshire. But Charlotte refused eligible offers of marriage and remained apparently heart-whole until in her travels she encountered the magnetic semi-charlatan Axel Munthe of *San Michele* fame. Munthe seems to have been the great physical love of her life and she made abject play for him, even to getting a pretty portrait of herself painted by the fashionable Sartorio as a present for him. Munthe evaded a commitment by not accepting the portrait, and it was left hanging about until the humiliated Charlotte reclaimed it. It ended up over the drawingroom mantelpiece in the Shaw country house at Ayot St Lawrence.

Whether Charlotte actually went to bed with Axel Munthe or even with her own husband is not known and is open to doubt. Her biographer Janet Dunbar professes the cosy belief that Charlotte and Shaw had a 'normal' married life, at least in the first years of their marriage. But St John Ervine, who was devoted to Charlotte in a filial way and knew her well, was convinced that she died a virgin. Ervine was old-fashioned enough to regard abstinence from carnal pleasure as a virtue in her. But little that we know of Charlotte suggests that she was the kind of person to deny herself any lawful pleasure that was available, and if she elected to remain celibate it was almost certainly because she had tried sexual intercourse and didn't like it. There is no reason to believe that she was lesbian. She was in fact very fond of the company of young men.

Charlotte's cousin, Edith Somerville of the famous Somerville and Ross writing team, summed up Charlotte with deadly accuracy: that she was *almost* clever but not quite. Charlotte was basically a kindly person, conscientiously honest and truthful in the disconcerting way Queen Victoria was, and she attracted much love. Her letters to her housekeeper show her as an amusing combination of mother and mother-superior but nevertheless explain the loyalty and devotion her servants accorded her. Again, like the young Victoria, she wished to be 'good', and to use her money to improve the world. The crack about Shaw being a good man fallen among Fabians could be more aptly applied to Charlotte, who fell among Sidney and Beatrice Webb. She began by asking them for advice on the best way to devote her surplus money to redeeming mankind. They promptly relieved her of a hefty contribution towards the expenses of founding the London School of Economics, which was duly opened on the ground floor of an elegant Adam house in the Adelphi, off the Strand, Charlotte taking the two upper storeys as a flat.

Beatrice, who was much given to organising people's lives for them whether they desired it or not, planned to marry off Charlotte to some needy Fabian who could live on her money while engineering the destruction of Charlotte's social class. Beatrice's candidate for the post was Graham Wallas: tall, good-looking, honourable, and a crushing bore. To provide opportunities for love-making she invited Graham Wallas to join them for a summer holiday in a country house she had rented. Shaw, as one of the Fabian inner cabinet, was included in the party as a matter of course. It would hardly have occurred to Beatrice that the weedy, talkative, restless journalist-playwright-street-corner-speaker with the poached-egg countenance could ever prove a rival to the splendid looking Wallas. If she thought about the matter at all it would have been to conclude complacently that the contrast between the two could only help Charlotte to make up her mind. It did. She fell for Shaw.

Charlotte, being still preoccupied by the reluctant Munthe, may not have realised quite how much she was being attracted to Shaw. They went out on cycling expeditions and Shaw, who all this time was writing almost daily letters to the actress Ellen Terry, reported to Ellen that he was getting very interested in his 'green-eyed Irish millionairess' and that the millionairess was responding. He put teasing questions to Ellen: should he fall in love with Miss P-T and marry her, thus getting hold of ever so many thousands a year? Ellen, divining that Miss P-T was not just another of Shaw's passing fancies, proffered the required encouragement.

Those daily letters to Ellen Terry require a word of explanation. Ellen had been made an ally by Shaw in his campaign to conquer the British theatre. His theatrical experience with Florence Farr had shown him how strong women's influence was in the theatre, not merely in filling seats but in forming managerial policy. Even when management to all appearances seemed firmly in male hands, the man could be manipulated through his woman, be she wife, mistress and/or leading lady. Shaw was simply following one of the most venerable and successful practices in politics and diplomacy: the first step towards squaring the ruler is to square the favourite. It was Ellen Terry herself who gave him his opportunity.

In 1892 she, then the undisputed queen of the London stage and Henry Irving's leading lady, wrote to Shaw to ask his opinion of a young girl singer-composer she was interested in. Shaw replied with an honest opinion which was not very encouraging for the young singer. Ellen Terry acknowledged his letter. He wrote again, Ellen again responded. He sent her a book he had published, presumably *The Quintessence of Ibsenism*, but there is no trace of a reply from her, and the correspondence lapsed. Then in March 1895 Ellen re-opened it with a note which was provoked by a newspaper item about a forthcoming talk of his to the Women's Progressive Society on the subject of 'Women's Meanness'. Ellen said she wished she could be there but that theatre work left her free only on Sunday nights. She asked to be let know if he ever lectured on Sundays as she would like to attend. The following November he notified her that he had just finished 'a beautiful little one-act play for Napoleon and a strange lady'. She took the hint,

inviting him to let her read it. Thus began his vigorous
cultivation of the goodwill of the Lyceum Theatre's
leading lady, in the course of which business tended
to become secondary to the affectionate pen-
friendship which soon developed. As Shaw was to
find out, Ellen Terry was a most lovable woman.
They wrote to each other, at times almost every day,
until his marriage to Charlotte began the inevitable
winding down of the correspondence.

The Napoleon play, *The Man of Destiny*, was
intended for Ellen Terry and Henry Irving, for Shaw
was planning to move from the Florence Farr/J. T.
Grein coterie theatre level to the top of the scale at
one step. But Irving didn't like the play and mistook
his man so far as to imagine that he could buy Shaw's
favour as a critic with the offer of a £50 option fee
for the piece, without having the least intention of
producing it. Shaw knew well what Irving was about.
If a critic didn't happen to have a play in his bottom
drawer there was always the alternative of the
advance payment for a translation from the French
which he could do at his leisure, the manager emphas-
ising that he was in no hurry for it. Bram Stoker,
Irving's literary manager and another Dubliner from
the old days, might well have suggested that the
offer be made.

Shaw, though outwardly polite, inwardly seethed
as he refused the option, and Irving was, of course,
furious at being rebuffed.

The truth is, Shaw had mixed feelings about Irving
as an actor. He resented, as an affront to the dramatist's dignity, the assumption Irving shared with almost
every other actor: that a play was merely the raw
material from which the actor fashioned a work of
art to suit his own taste and resources. Irving's
insensitive cuts in Shakespeare, whom he professed
to worship, greatly angered Shaw, all the more so as

they were not made just to bring the plays within conventional time-limits but to enable Irving to sub- stitute elaborate stage spectacle for the verse. Again, Shaw was contemptuous of Irving's efforts to secure vocal resonance by using his nose as an echo chamber. This was a double wound. Irving's nose was almost equine in its prominence, although Shaw may not have had this in mind when writing of his 'whinnying'.

Above all there was Irving's lofty disregard of contemporary drama. Not only did he ignore Ibsen and favour the mock-Elizabethan blank verse dramas of Tennyson, Comyns Carr and W. G. Wills (a Dublin born painter and writer who was related to Oscar Fingal O'Flahertie Wills Wilde) but he was neglecting opportunities to repent and reform by embracing the new Shavian drama.

Shaw gaily admitted that he had personal reasons for allowing Irving no quarter. He claimed that both were bitter rivals for Ellen Terry's love, a claim that amused Ellen but would have irritated Irving by its impertinent assumption of equality of status with him. Not that Ellen and Shaw hadn't grown fond of each other, but the romance remained strictly epistolary and they made a point, as Tchaikovsky and Nadejda von Meck did, of not meeting in the flesh. Neither could they disguise their delight as connoisseurs of performance in putting on a show for each other. But although Shaw made plentiful use of love language, it was all so lighthearted that Ellen could go on receiving such advances, even giving guarded encouragement, without having the uncomfortable feeling that she was committing herself in any serious way or that the affair might get out of hand as was to happen later with Shaw and Mrs Pat Campbell. This was why Shaw was able to inform Ellen of his growing interest in Charlotte without giving offence, and why Ellen was able to encourage him without incurring the suspicion of feeling put out.

He had also ventilated to Ellen his awareness of how vulnerable he was to the imputation of being a fortune hunter, while delicately intimating that he was himself no longer penniless. For the actor-manager Richard Mansfield had become interested in his plays and ran them in America, scoring a lucrative success with *The Devil's Disciple*, a play about America's independence struggle which American audiences could view with no small complacency. Shaw told Ellen Terry that by investing his initial royalties in county council stock he could assure himself of £20 a year for his old age, adding the teasing threat that he would take a theatre presently and engage Irving for eccentric comedy. The bubbling fun of such utterances concealed the alarming deterioration in his health, just as the celestially youthful score of *The Magic Flute* concealed the same kind of thing in Mozart's, and if he escaped Mozart's fate it was only by the skin of his teeth.

His activity at this time, his daily outpouring of words for articles, letters, publicity paragraphs, the endless lectures and debates on the evenings he hadn't to go to the theatre, suggest not a healthful abundance of energy but nervous frenzy. Charlotte had gone off to Italy to have another try at Munthe, and Shaw was pursuing her with daily letters. To see the original letters is to gain a different impression from reading them in print. He was scribbling on odds and ends of paper, including slips from a small day-by-day calandar, the paper covered with writing from edge to edge, sometimes turning corners and climbing up the side. One senses that he was at the end of his tether. He himself seems to have realised this and in fact, as he was afterwards to admit, believed he had not much longer to live. One sister had died at twenty, the survivor was not robust.

It looked as if none of GCS's children would equal his three score years and ten.

His mother was another worry. She was sixty-eight and though in splendid preservation and still able to earn her living, it could not be long in the nature of things before she had to give up and rely on him for her support. She also had a corps of half-sisters who, orphaned like herself by the death of the Carlow squire, were wistfully waiting for whatever crumbs fell from her table. Bessie had been both widowed and orphaned in 1885, GCS dying in April and Walter Bagenal Gurly in December, aged eighty-five. Yet although Shaw was her son and her insurance policy, Bessie took as little care of him as ever, pursuing her unnoticing way, wrapped up in her own affairs, such concern as she could spare for others being concentrated on her daughter. Her son was let look after himself in almost everything except the meals of eggs, bread and cocoa the maid of all work served to him when he was at home.

A bad situation became worse when he developed a foot infection, attributed to a too-tightly laced boot, which caused considerable swelling and required surgical operations on a bone. The operations were performed by Salisbury Sharpe, husband of Shaw's old flame Alice Lockett, and were successful. The breakdown obliged him to give up the *Saturday Review* job, which he was intending to do anyway, partly because Frank Harris was in arrears with payment but chiefly because, given a little luck and provided his health held out, he could make a four-figure income from theatre royalties.

Meanwhile if Bessie did not realise how near the grave he was, others did. Word was sent to Charlotte about his condition and she, apparently acknowledging to herself that she could never catch Munthe, turned for home. She took her time, making an unscheduled stop in Paris and bitterly disappointing him by still not being there when he hobbled around to her Adelphi Terrace flat for a lovers' reunion. But at long last she arrived in London and on going to see him at Fitzroy Square was horrified to find him in such squalor and so alarmingly frail.

His account of what happened next is the usual comic exaggeration. She is supposed to have announced that she would carry him off to a house in the country, where she would nurse him back to health. He is supposed to have refused to endanger the good name of Fabianism by living alone with an unmarried lady. Therefore before she can save him she has to go out to buy a wedding ring and a licence and bear him off to a registry office. Bride and groom then separate, returning to their respective dwellings.

Charlotte did not contradict this obviously unlikely tale. Not the least of her virtues as a mate for Bernard Shaw was that on this occasion, and for the rest of their married life, she let him do all the talking. As a result we are never embarrassed by conflicts in their evidence and we can never be sure of the facts. No doubt she did have to go out and buy the ring and the licence, for he was in no fit state to do anything that could be done for him by somebody else. But as to whether he formally proposed or she gallantly volunteered, we can only guess. The sole indisputable fact is that on 1 June 1898 George Bernard Shaw and Charlotte Payne-Townshend were married in the Strand Registry Office, Henry Salt and Graham Wallas being the witnesses. Shaw alleged that by wearing a jacket made ragged by his crutches he was mistaken for a beggar while the imposing Wallas, dressed in his best, was taken to be the groom. Only that Wallas hesitated over a formula that seemed a bit strong for a mere witness he would have found himself with an unexpected wife. (Second wife, strictly speaking, for he had married another lady who, if not quite as well endowed financially as Charlotte, had some money.)

Since all this was published in newspaper paragraphs supplied by the semi-anonymous groom, it is not surprising that Charlotte's conventionally respectable sister, Cissy, was aghast to find such a brother-in-law had been inflicted upon her. She refused point blank to meet him or have any communication with him, and for some years there was bad feeling between the sisters. But when Cissy eventually got to know Shaw, while she may not have actually come to love him or to accept him in spite of the family baronet, she at least came to tolerate him, receiving him as a guest in her house, going on trips abroad with him and Charlotte, and finally allowing him to dedicate to her his monumental *Intelligent Woman's Guide to Socialism and Capitalism*.

So far as we know, neither Shaw nor Charlotte ever made a concrete and unambiguous statement to anyone else about any conditions that might have been laid down about the physical side of their relationship. In the so-called 'Sex Credo' letter to Frank Harris, which Shaw allowed – in fact *arranged* – to be published in Harris's biography of him, he states that 'sex had no part' in his relations with Charlotte, and since Charlotte was very much alive and alert at the time her silence on the revelation may be taken as confirming its truth. We must also conclude that she was in no way ashamed or embarrassed by the revelation because we can be sure that Shaw would never have published anything hurtful to her, especially on so personal and delicate a matter.

What Charlotte's intentions were at the time she agreed to marry him we do not know. She was well into her forty-second year, and may have been in the middle of her menopause with all its attendant emotional disturbances, so that a distaste for copulation could have been merely temporary. If, as so often happens, a temporary arrangement drifts into a permanent one, then the same question can be asked about the Shaws as is so often asked about nuns and the celibate clergy: a question to which we are never given a straight answer from the only people in a position to give it.

At any rate Charlotte appears to have been free from any desire to reproduce her kind, and indeed referred to babies in general as 'horrid little things'. I happened to attend a meeting of the Shaw Society in London at which Blanche Patch, Shaw's secretary for thirty years, was present, and I asked her what she thought of St John Ervine's belief that the Shaws were not married in the usual sense of that term. She replied, naturally enough, that she knew nothing about that side of their life, that they were already elderly when she first knew them, that they then had separate bedrooms but that no one who saw them together could doubt for a moment that they loved each other very much. She had often seen Mr Shaw greeting Charlotte with a most affectionate embrace. They were completely at ease with each other and would sit side by side on a couch like Darby and Joan, and Charlotte loved him to read to her and sing for her (which he did right up to the end), and no wife could have wished for a more solicitous or attentive husband. All the other evidence points to this being the simple truth of the matter, at any rate during the final quarter century of their marriage. The first twenty years, however, were not quite so idyllic. Too many of Shaw's women friends and acquaintances seemed ready to offer the services that Charlotte may have been withholding and Shaw was not repulsing them as brusquely as Charlotte would have wished.

2

Marriage changed Shaw's lifestyle more than his [101] life because his life was his work. Even if Charlotte had not been willing to accept this there was little she could have done about it. As things were, she was happy in being married to a genius and felt, as Bessie had felt forty years earlier, that her empty life had been filled, that at last she had a cause and a creed. She accordingly dedicated herself to the production, development and preservation of the genius as ardently as Bessie had done for the voice. It need hardly be said that Bessie and Lucy detested her, visits and other social contacts being kept to the irreducible minimum. They called her Carlotta, which was something of a private joke. In Dublin, near Synge Street, there is a Charlotte Street which, being named in honour of George III's German consort, was by old Dubliners pronounced German-fashion, Carlotta Street. Shaw was always George to his mother and sister, although he hated being Georged; he had a clause in his contracts with theatre managers stipulating that the George was to be omitted from his name in billings and advertisements. Spice was added to the George-Carlotta jest by the fact that the street consisted of small seedy shops, with the kerbsides taken over by hawkers and flower sellers.

Shaw let them have their little joke, and by taking no notice of it ensured that nobody else would notice it either. He categorically stated that he got Charlotte to make a marriage settlement under which, should he pre-decease his mother, she and Lucy would receive a small income. This was to save them from having to beg from the despised Carlotta. But research has uncovered no record of any financial arrangement of this kind.

Before his marriage at the age of forty-two he had known only by observation but not by experience what it is like to live on an assured, adequate income in a comfortable and well-ordered household, where the wife at least goes through the motions of respecting her husband, making his personal comfort her anxious concern, and not openly preferring a lame magnetic singing teacher to him. As from his wedding day he became a pampered husband, never being obliged to yield precedence to anyone or anything under his own roof or having to worry about providing money to pay the household bills or his wife's dressmaker's account, freed for life from any uncomfortable speculations as to whether he would end up in rags in the gutter. The newly married Charlotte's first care had been to bear him off to a rented country house in Surrey where there was no longer any danger of his dying 'of a deficiency of servants'. When his foot began to mend nicely he fell on the stairs and broke an arm, fortunately not the writing one. But whether a tumble left him still able to pick himself up or obliged him to wait for somebody to come and do the job for him, he never let it interfere with his daily output of written words. When he was too tired or too ill to hold a pen, he dictated, and here again Charlotte often filled the role of amanuensis.

In a word, marriage to Charlotte marked the end of hack journalism (hack, that is, by Shavian standards) and brought the freedom to concentrate time and energy on the kind of work he believed himself best fitted for. The result was that for a couple of years after his marriage his income as an author fell although his output of words remained high. Here are some of his tax returns:

1894/5   Books £3; Journalism £293. 17. 3; Plays £568. 0. 4½.

1895/6	Books £1. 10. 6. (*Quintessence of Ibsenism*); Journalism £398; Plays £93. 15. 0.	[103]
1898	£2378. 11. 3.	
1898/9	£473. 5. 11.	
1899/1900	£313. 11. 0.	
1901	£474. 8. 7.	
1901/2	£90. 8. 0.	

The tax inspector might have concluded with a cynical smile that here was yet another honest worker who had been demoralised by marriage to a wealthy woman. The truth is that in the apparently fallow couple of years he had embarked on the series of plays that made him the greatest playwright of his time, second only to Shakespeare in the English-speaking theatre. Seldom has an author been so blessed with good luck at just the right moment in his career or, it may be added, been so little spoiled by it.

3

The first product of his improved living conditions was *Caesar and Cleopatra*, an essay in the epic style, written with Forbes-Robertson and Mrs Pat Campbell in mind, their stars being then in the ascendant and Irving's and Ellen Terry's in decline. Caesar was Shaw painting his own portrait through rose-coloured spectacles. The self-identification with the great Roman is frank and unabashed. Endowed with absolute power, Shaw-Caesar shows little sign of tending to be corrupted absolutely. A more amiable and courtly dictator would be hard to find. True, this Caesar has not been completely without sin, but the sins were committed in the heat of the moment in earlier years and are now sincerely repented of. His colleagues stand in awe of his natural superiority but are saved by his reassuring geniality from being overawed. Woman is again the pursuer but Shaw-Caesar virtually advises her to go and have a cold shower. Not even when alone with a sex-kitten Cleopatra in a moonlit desert does he experience any impulse towards doing what comes naturally: he remains paternal, serene, philosophical. You could use the score of Mozart's *Clemency of Titus* as incidental music for *Caesar and Cleopatra* without any incongruity.

Wisely Shaw doesn't try conclusions with Shakespeare on Shakespeare's own ground. There is no attempt to offer us a rival portrait of the mature Cleopatra. He gives us the schoolgirl, not yet able to understand experienced men or to cope with them. In a word, where it comes to dramatising the Conqueror of Gaul and the Serpent of the Old Nile, Dublin has to yield the palm to Stratford-on-Avon. Nevertheless when all is said and done, *Caesar and Cleopatra* remains a fine play in its class and will fully justify the heavy cost of producing it with the splendour of setting and costume for which it calls.

Surprisingly, many plays that Shaw wrote for specific performers were not hungrily seized by them and staged without a moment's avoidable delay. Thus it was with *Caesar and Cleopatra*. Another such case was *Captain Brassbound's Conversion*, which was written, with high hopes, for Ellen Terry. But that actress read the manuscript with a lacklustre eye and somewhat coolly returned it to the, unusually for him, deeply wounded author, who wrote to Ellen on 4 August 1899:

> Alas, dear Ellen, is it really so? Then I can do nothing for you. I honestly thought that Lady Cicely would fit you like a glove.

Ellen later saw the light and produced *Brassbound* under her own management with some success.

Caesar and Cleopatra was not performed in London until 1907 when Forbes-Robertson had noted from the success of the famous Royal Court Theatre season that Shaw could be 'box-office' after all.

Shaw's next rebuff came from a quarter that was at once surprising and yet not in the least surprising: his native Dublin. As will be recalled, *Arms and the Man* had been more successful with audiences than Yeats's *Land of Heart's Desire* and Dr Todhunter's *Comedy of Sighs* during Florence Farr's short season at the Avenue Theatre in London in 1894, although it must have been some comfort to Yeats to have supplanted Shaw in Florence Farr's affections soon afterwards. By 1904 Yeats and Lady Gregory, Edward Martyn and George Moore had got the Abbey Theatre off the ground and were looking for new plays of Irish interest. Yeats knew that Shaw had for some years been mulling over a theme for a play about the Irish and the English, and, to spur him into getting it down on paper, invited him to write a play for the Abbey. Shaw responded with *John Bull's Other Island*. One would imagine that anyone capable of distinguishing between *Hamlet* and *Charley's Aunt* would have recognised *John Bull's Other Island* as destined to be a crown jewel of the Abbey's repertoire. But Yeats turned it down with flimsy excuses about not having the resources for it. This was nearly as disgraceful an act as his later rejection of Seán O'Casey's *Silver Tassie*, and it can be said to the credit of Yeats's eventual successor at the Abbey, the much despised dethroned politician Ernest Blythe, that although Blythe turned away some plays he should have produced he never perpetrated two such crass literary blunders as did the poet of Innisfree. Even though *John Bull's Other Island* was not the kind of play likely to appeal personally to the author of *The Land of Heart's*

Desire and *Cathleen Ni Houlihan*, common civility as between one author and another required that Yeats should produce the play he had solicited (without any commissioning fee or advance of royalties), unless it proved technically inept or artistically shoddy. Moreover, Yeats as an author would have known what labour has to be expended in creating so substantial a piece as *John Bull*, which makes his snooty rejection of it all the more deplorable. Strong words, these, which one would refrain from applying to a lesser man. But from those to whom much has been given, much is expected. Yeats should have known better.

Many guesses have been made at the identity of the model for the representative Englishman in the play, Tom Broadbent. Winston Churchill has so far not been included in the list. But in January 1904 he visited Dublin, or rather re-visited it, having lived there as a young boy when his grandfather, the Duke of Marlborough, was Viceroy. During his 1904 visit Winston was guest of honour at a dinner given by the Corinthian Club, and in replying to the toast to him made a speech in pure Broadbentese. For example, 'I feel as St Patrick must have felt when he landed to convert the Irish nation. I can only hope that I may have, if not the good fortune St Patrick had, at any rate some proportion of that good fortune in driving out of Ireland the fiscal frogs and tariff toads.' Some lines of his speech are actually appropriated for Broadbent. 'I am very grateful to you for your kindness in allowing me to come here tonight and for the very friendly manner in which you have drunk my health . . . (*Laughter and 'Hear! Hear!'*).'

John Bull's Other Island was first produced in London, at the Royal Court Theatre, where it enjoyed resounding success. Arthur Balfour, who had been Chief Secretary of Ireland (in effect, prime minister of the country), returned to see it again and again, bringing political friends in the hope of enlightening them on the Irish Question. He got Edward VII, who was fond of playgoing, to come. Edward's reaction was typical of Shaw's audiences then and for many years afterwards: he broke his chair in a convulsion of laughter and retained his old opinion that the author was quite mad, a view formed after seeing *Arms and the Man*. Yet in spite of *John Bull's* success and of the author's fame, Shaw was still finding it hard to get a real foothold in the London theatre, to achieve something of the respect accorded to men like Arthur Pinero and the egregious Henry Arthur Jones, who, friendly enough so long as Shaw was trailing far behind him, went bonkers when overtaken. Shaw therefore fell back on publication in book form as the only available method of introducing his plays to the public. In the Spring of 1898 he got Grant Richards, not the least enterprising of publishers, to issue two volumes of them. They were called *Plays Pleasant* and *Plays Unpleasant* and were notable for the intelligent and attractive way they were prepared for the reader. The stage directions, instead of being mere bald specifications of exits and entrances, were proffered in narrative form, just as in a novel, and character sketches were included, many of Dickensian brilliance and penetration.

These character sketches are invaluable to the actor who has enough brains to be able to use them, and to the director who has brains enough to *let* the actor use them. More than one director has said to me that when Shaw's stage directions are followed there can never be any confusion in the staging, with actors 'masking' one another or not being in the right place when required: a tribute that cannot be paid to all dramatic authors.

[108] By a stroke of dramatic irony Henry Irving died as Shaw entered upon his kingdom with the Vedrenne-Barker seasons at the Royal Court Theatre. Irving had been in failing health since the turn of the century, partly because of exhaustion brought about by the intensity of his acting, partly because of his heavy smoking, not then recognised as a menace to heart and lung. After a performance in Bradford as Becket in Tennyson's play, he drove to his hotel and dropped dead in the foyer. The ever faithful Bram Stoker, to whom he was a god, was at his side.

The sudden death at sixty-seven of a former darling of the public aroused one of those waves of sympathy and sentiment which such events usually create, and warn those who may not have a good word to say about the departed to hold off until the funeral wreaths begin to wither. Shaw was once again the exception that proved the rule. In private he did what he could to facilitate Irving's burial in Westminster Abbey: Irving's wife had long been estranged from him and in her bitterness she was prepared to object to a tomb in the Abbey, which would have caused scandal. Shaw soothed her into silence by pointing out that a scandal would jeopardise her chance of a civil list pension. But Shaw refused an invitation to attend the funeral for the snooty reason that Literature had no place at Irving's graveside. This naturally caused offence and was talked about, enabling Shaw to upstage the actor at his own funeral. Nor was this the end of the affair. A Viennese paper, *Die Neue Freie Presse*, invited him to write an obituary appreciation. He responded with a well-expressed and justifiably critical evaluation to which no one could have objected had it appeared when Irving was some time in his tomb. But in the circumstances, apparently harsh criticism was news. The *Neue Freie*

Presse article, which had been translated into German, was re-translated into English by some anonymous hand and much distorted in the process. Shaw had pointed out how Irving was interested only in himself, this being an imaginary self in an imaginary world. 'He lived in a dream.' The re-translated translations appeared in the English papers as: 'He was a narrow-minded egoist, devoid of culture, and living on the dream of his own greatness.' Not that even this version was totally unjustified, but the harshness of expression shocked people who believed that decent reticence should be observed at least until the corpse is cold. Shaw immediately offered the newspapers a copy of his original article as a free contribution, but only one editor availed himself of the offer. Editors are, as a race, less interested in truth than in 'news', and prefer the exciting slant to the hard fact. Shaw became unpopular for a while, and an attempt was made by some of those officiously righteous persons that are always with us, to prevent him speaking at a public meeting quite unconnected with Irving.

Meanwhile Ellen Terry, in deep distress, had written to him:

You never wrote the words they say you wrote, except when Henry was well, was at work and *fighting*. Then it was all right enough — fair. You never said it I am sure when all his friends were sore and smarting. *You* don't add hyssop to the wounds . . . Did he have faults? Yes! But of course *we* have none! I'm far away in the North and have only just heard that you were unkind. I don't believe that. I suppose time will bring me printed matter. When it comes I shall have no eyes to read with. I couldn't *cry* and something seemed to fix my eyes open and strain them. I feel badly. I'm sorry because I didn't do enough whilst I could, just a little longer.

Here we have Ellen Terry at her magnificent best. As Shaw was to remark many years afterwards her words are Irving's most precious epitaph. His reply on 28 October 1905 was a rather laboured explanation of how his original comments came to be distorted, a response so far from easing Ellen's hurt that she turned uncharacteristically snappish:

> Well, it was stupid in you, that's all — and that's enough I should say for *you*. I can't understand how one without gross food in him, who takes no wine to befuddle his wits, can have been so indelicate. Nothing is expected of *me*, or most of us, but of you I expect everything.

5

The Royal Court Theatre had been built in 1888 on the site of an older theatre, itself a badly transformed nonconformist chapel. Being out of the way for the general run of West End theatregoers, it fell on hard times and was leased by a rich businessman, J. H. Leigh. He had a passion for acting, shared by his young wife (who had been his ward), and staged some Shakespearean plays in which he and she took part. When ambition had been satisfied for the moment, Leigh allowed his manager, John Eugene Vedrenne, in collaboration with a handsome young actor-director, Harley Granville Barker, to use the Court for staging some 'uncommercial drama'. Vedrenne-Barker started with six matinées of *Candida*, another Shaw play which had been on the shelf since being performed by the Stage Society some years previously. It had one virtually impossible part, that of the Shelleyan young poet Eugene Marchbanks, competitor with Candida's husband for her love, looking the complete weakling but having a stronger character than the manly husband. Barker seemed to have been created specially for the role. He looked the other-world artist to his fingertips: all soul and sensibility, and slim. Shaw and Charlotte, who had come across him at the Stage Society productions, were much taken by him and were all for his directing *Candida* and playing the poet, although Shaw conscientiously warned him that the whole enterprise would prove 'a hideous folly'. It didn't. It was a success. Not even the finicky author found fault with Barker as director or actor.

Those who imagine that the great metropolis of London would not stoop to the kind of spinsterish gossip that Dublin specialises in may be surprised to learn that it was confidently reported that Barker was Shaw's son. People believed they could detect resemblances. In no way could Barker's elegant countenance be described as like an imperfectly poached egg but he did have reddish hair, was pale, and at this stage of his life hadn't a pick on him. Above all there was Shaw's obvious affection for him, and his unconscious habit of staring at him during rehearsals with a 'that's-my-boy' expression. But the allegation of paternity was utterly unfounded.

Other plays by other authors, including Galsworthy, Gilbert Murray, and Barker himself, were produced by the Vedrenne-Barker partnership, every production achieving some meausre of distinction and success. Shaw was not officially part of the Court management but interfered and intervened as if he were. Barker did not openly resent these trespassings, partly because of his genuine respect and liking for Shaw, partly no doubt because of his no less genuine respect and liking for Charlotte's purse. (She had secretly contributed to the financing of the partnership, something her husband might have guessed without being told. But one sometimes suspects that like other husbands Shaw used a Nelsonian eye when it suited him.) Vedrenne was not the man to mind very much who did what so long as no charge was being made. He was, as Barker said, 'the most cautious of men', always knowing to a shilling where he was and always ensuring that every shilling brought its shilling's worth, and more. Shaw didn't shrink from playing one off against the other in his Irish way, sympathising with the extravagant Barker over Vedrenne's stinginess and agreeing with Vedrenne that Barker mustn't be let bankrupt them all with his expensive demands.

But between the three of them they changed the face of British drama in a relatively short period, 1904-7, bringing Shaw to the forefront as a dramatist and laying the foundation for his eventual fortune.

John Bull's Other Island (originally entitled *Rule, Britannia*) was presented at a matinee on 1 November 1904, Shaw producing and Barker playing Peter Keegan the unfrocked priest. The success of this production has already been mentioned. Then in May 1905 came *Man and Superman* which, although played without its third act and the celebrated Hell scene, caused the words Shaw and genius to be conjoined by the perceptive. The part of Ann Whitefield was played by the beautiful but respectable Lillah McCarthy, who presently married Barker, receiving from the Shaws a wedding present of a Bechstein piano with pianola attachment.

Barker, made up to look like Shaw, played John Tanner, but his quiet, restrained, totally unoperatic style would not have allowed him make the most of this wonderful role, which is Don Giovanni with brains and a social conscience, pursued by women not pursuing them. A much better Tanner was the flamboyant Robert Loraine who brought the play to America, making it the smash hit of the New York season and allegedly breaking the box-office record of the Ziegfeld Follies.

While *Man and Superman* was making Shaw's fortune in America, he had provided the Court with another masterpiece, *Major Barbara*, an effective sermon on the Butlerian text of look after the money and your morals will then look after themselves. The play was embellished with excellent portraits of Professor Gilbert Murray and his mother-in-law the Countess of Carlisle as Adolphus Cusins and Lady Britomart.

All in all 1905 was a notable year for Shaw. He had amply tasted real fame and real fortune. He also returned to Ireland for a holiday (July-September), his first glimpse of his native land since leaving it thirty years previously. He alleged that he had made the journey merely to please Charlotte, who wanted to see her old home at Rosscarbery once again. He was not entirely at his ease. The play he was working on during his 'holiday,' *Major Barbara*, proved troublesome and he blamed this on the uncongenial atmosphere of Ireland. He had to re-write a large part of the play on returning to England, one of the few occasions on which such radical revision was necessary with him.

The following year saw the production of *The Doctor's Dilemma*, in which the *concerto grosso* passages for the doctors (shades of Uncle Walter) constitute scenes of delectable high comedy that age cannot wither nor custom stale. Unlike *Major Barbara*, this play came easily, taking only a month in the writing. Its successor, *Getting Married*, is a conversation piece about the pros and cons of marriage as an institution. One character, Mrs George (!), wife of a greengrocer who also 'undertakes' wedding breakfasts, has the faculty of going into trances in [114] which she makes speeches in Shaw's poetic prose vein, a reminder that Bessie had a somewhat similar faculty, producing while in her trances a series of elaborate 'spirit drawings'.

In publishing his plays Shaw developed the explanatory prefaces of his first two volumes into lengthy disquisitions, more or less related to the play. He advised people to read the play first, then the preface. This was sound advice. Some of the prefaces are not only longer than the play but require more intense concentration from the reader than the play from the spectator. In fact at the time the prefaces seemed more important than the plays and a Shaw preface became a much sought after thing in itself. Time has eroded much of the importance of the prefaces, events having caught up with them. The causes they campaigned for – a national health service, the concession of home rule to colonies, easier divorce, more humane upbringing of children, abolition of ritual flogging, and so on – have since been won. Other causes have become dead ducks, at least for the moment: the desirability of Caesarean dictatorship, the need for more extensive liquidation of undesirables who cannot adapt themselves to Utopian conditions. There are also one or two causes which have been won but did not turn out quite so well as Shaw had led us to believe they would. National theatres, for example.

During the years leading to World War I the flow of plays and playlets continued steadily. *Fanny's First Play*, on the age-old theme of the rebellion of the rising generation against its predecessor, was produced anonymously, because it contains scenes which do for the dramatic critics what *The Doctor's Dilemma* did for the medicos, though not quite so amusingly. Shaw, the ex-critic, was increasingly restless over being so much at the receiving end, and blamed persistently bad notices for the tragic failure of the Vedrenne-Barker enterprise in the end. He eased his feelings by caricaturing his oppressors, though without cruelty. Trotter (A. B. Walkley) is the best of the caricatures, perhaps because Walkley was the most interesting subject. He was in on the secret of the author's identity, and good-naturedly went backstage to help with the make-up of the actor impersonating him.

The anonymity of *Fanny's First Play* aroused enough curiosity to bring audiences rolling in for two and a half years. It was, incidentally, the only play of his which Shaw helped to finance. *Fanny* was put on under the managership of Lillah McCarthy, whose marriage was not prospering, much to the dismay of the Shaws. He provided her with half the £1000 capital, Lord Howard de Walden with the other half.

The Vedrenne-Barker venture came to an end in 1907, the uncommercial drama proving truly uncommercial when, the Court lease having run out, the partners tried their luck with the big time at the Savoy Theatre. To extricate them from the disgrace of bankruptcy, Shaw handed back most of the money they had made for him, and Barker was left penniless.

6

The ending of the Vedrenne-Barker facility meant that Shaw no longer had what was in effect his own festival theatre. Of the thousand or so performances given at the Court, three-quarters had been of Shaw plays, with the author allowed to direct rehearsals when convenient for him, Barker capably taking over when it was not. Shaw now had to return to cultivating the favour of big actor-managers and coaxing the temperamental *prime donne* who pulled in the cash customers. This is how he came to aim his flatteries towards Mrs Pat Campbell and to manoeuvre her into appearing in the apparently grotesquely unsuitable role of a Cockney flowergirl, opposite the no less temperamental Herbert Beerbohm Tree, lord of the vast His Majesty's Theatre and Irving's acknowledged successor as monarch of the British stage.

Mrs Pat's first reaction to the flowergirl was outrage, or at least a show of it. She allowed the author to read the play to her and then vamped him sufficiently to convince him that he had hooked her. The play was, of course, *Pygmalion*, in which the theme of using phonetics to pass off a guttersnipe as a duchess was treated in counterpoint with that of the changing human relations between pupil and teacher. Its Cinderella aspect has given it its great and lasting appeal. The idea of a play about a working-class girl in a hat with orange and red feathers, who becomes involved with a West End gentleman, had occurred to Shaw as far back as 1897 when he was working on *Caesar and Cleopatra*. It wasn't taken up by him in earnest until 1912, when it was completed in three months.

Shaw described himself as emerging from the task of rehearsing *Pygmalion* like an old dog which has got the worst of a fight. This was the truth but not the whole truth. The temperamental stars had given him a hard time sure enough, but he had complicated the situation by falling in love with Mrs Pat. He was fifty-seven and she forty-eight, and they conducted themselves with all the idiocy to be expected of a pair of exhibitionists who at that time of life keep capering around the bed but not getting into it. Shaw chattered all over London about how he had been bewitched, provoking Sidney Webb (shrilly certified by Beatrice to the the perfect lover by night and by day) into diagnosing a case of sexual senility. Mrs Pat, as a woman, had to be more discreet. She took to visiting Lucy, partly to annoy Shaw, who didn't want to be talked about by his sister (he warned Mrs Pat that Lucy would tell her lies about his childhood), and partly because it gave Shaw an opportunity to meet her there without scandal.

Lucy, who was just as experienced a warrior-queen of romance as Mrs Pat, must have known perfectly well what the visits were all about. St John Ervine declares that Lucy's dislike of Charlotte would have added zest to her enjoyment of her part in deceiving Charlotte, and it is impossible to pooh-pooh this completely. But Lucy was in an awkward situation. She and her home were being maintained at Shaw's expense, so that she could hardly forbid his visits even if she wanted to. Far from wanting to do this she welcomed any excuse that brought him to the house, for his visits had become rarer since the death of their mother in the February of that year (1913).

One wonders whether Bessie's death had upset Shaw far more than he had let on, so that his sudden importuning of Mrs Pat had something in it of a deep need for consolation. He had indulged in some play-acting at Bessie's funeral, inviting Barker to be the only mourner apart from himself and bringing him around behind the scenes at the crematorium to witness the actual pushing of the coffin into the furnace. They had then gone for a walk around Golders Green and done some shopping until it was time to return to the crematorium to see two attendants sorting out Bessie's ashes from the remnants of her coffin. He told Barker that he felt his mother was looking over his shoulder at the operation and talking to him. A really unfeeling person would not have gone on like this but would have taken care to hide lack of emotion behind conventional solemnity. Shaw was not the most demonstrative of sons, for Bessie, no gusher, never encouraged shows of affection even when her children were very young. But few men remain unmoved by their mother's death and nothing we know of Shaw entitles us to include him in those few.

He wrote an account of the funeral to Mrs Pat, saying that he had chosen to unburden himself to her because *she* didn't hate her mother and even didn't hate her children. 'You mother was not the Enemy.' Bessie's pulverised ashes were scattered on a flower bed. Five days later he was addressing endearments to Mrs Pat who was now, amongst other things, his Virgin Mother enthroned in heaven. The following day she got a seven-verse parody of Cock Robin:

> Who clasped her tight?
> That wasn't right.
> Oh, the delight!
> *I* clasped her tight.

Mrs Pat could respond in kind and, when rattled, could strike to wound:

> You vagabond you — you blind man. You weaver of words, you — black and purple winged hider of cherubs — you poor thing unable to understand a mere woman. My friend all the same. No daughters to relieve your cravings — no babes to stop your satirical chatterings, why should I pay for all your shortcomings. You in your broom-stick and sheet have crackers and ashes within you —

What had rattled her was that early in August Mrs Pat felt he was destabilising the situation and confessed as much to him.

Its [*sic*] getting difficult not to love you more than
I ought to love you — Offend me again quickly to [119]
pull me together — But by the sea I must be alone
— you know.

She went to Sandwich and he, sexually aroused,
followed her and checked in at the same hotel. She
dealt with this ticklish situation by leading him to
assume they would be together the following morning.
But when morning came he found she had fled back
to London, leaving him to send after her one of the
bitterest letters he ever penned. 'La ci darem' had
changed to 'La vendetta'.

Both were at fault, she more than he in so far as
she had deliberately led him on. Her behaviour was
all the shabbier since she was arranging to marry a
younger man than Shaw, George Cornwallis-West,
formerly second husband of Winston Churchill's
mother. Shaw was aware of her engagement. In fact
he met Cornwallis-West, and found that they both
took to each other. But he made an undignified plea
to Mrs Pat not to marry his rival for a while, he being
young and therefore better able to wait for the prize
than himself. Mrs Pat married Cornwallis-West a few
days before the opening of *Pygmalion* in April 1914,
disappearing on honeymoon in the middle of dress
rehearsals.

Pygmalion made Shaw a popular author as distinct
from a famous one, and probably would have run for
ever if World War I hadn't broken out in August and
put an end to West End theatre for the moment. The
Higgins, Beerbohm Tree, half brother of the
incomparable Max whom Shaw had installed as his
successor at the *Saturday Review*, wasn't satisfactory.
Being the proprietor-manager of His Majesty's
Theatre as well as its star, he wasn't so easily to be
directed in the way the author wished him to go as

had been Barker in the Court Theatre days. Thus he insisted on imposing a 'happy ending' on the piece by implying that Eliza would marry Higgins instead of Freddy. There can be no question that this is what the audience wants, and will continue to want so long as the casting of the two chief parts does not underline that Eliza is a teenager and Higgins is in his forties and that a romance between them is an unpleasant reflection upon Higgins's character. But rare indeed is the production in which this difference is made clear. Even in the famous film version, for which Shaw vainly sought to have Charles Laughton cast as Higgins, the age gap between Wendy Hiller and Leslie Howard was hardly noticeable, so that the failure of romance to blossom between them seemed inexplicable to audiences except by reason of Higgins being a homosexual, a thing nowhere suggested in the text. A fair question would be: why didn't Shaw stress the age gap in the text when half a dozen lines could put the matter beyond question? Two answers suggest themselves. First, it would have been tactless to do this when Mrs Pat was forty-nine and Tree a touchy sixty-one, with the credulity of the audience being already strained to accept her as a teenager. Secondly, since the Eliza-Higgins story closely paralleled that of Bessie and Vandeleur Lee, Shaw instinctively shrank from marrying them off in the end.

These considerations apart, the play is far more effective, more convincing, more touching when the age gap is made clear and the father-teacher and daughter-pupil relationships are emphasised rather than that of Cinderella and Prince Charming.

On the outbreak of war Mrs Pat migrated to America with *Pygmalion*, and Shaw, convinced that his pen was mightier than any sword, addressed himself to the task of stopping the war single-handed.

He had already for some years been warning against the stupidity and folly of war, and had brought himself to believe that Sir Edward Grey, the Foreign Secretary, was deliberately fomenting a European conflict. He now published a long article *Commonsense About the War* as a supplement to the recently founded *New Statesman*, which had been brought into existence by the Webbs as a Fabian organ, Shaw contributing £1,000 to the venture. Seventy-five thousand copies of *Commonsense* were sold. An impressive figure when considered in isolation, its significance is lessened when the 1914 population of Britain — over 40 million — is taken into account. Seventy-five thousand copies were not enough to make much impact upon the public at large, who in any event were not given to reading long articles even by so entertaining an author as Shaw. But the effect of *Commonsense* was as if Shaw had personally insulted virtually everybody in the island.

What happened was that the news editors of the popular press, always on the watch for a sensation, decided that Shaw's thesis could be tortured into one. Briefly, Shaw maintained that England had been preparing for war just like the Germans, that Grey was an English Junker hell bent on maintaining British supremacy in the balance-of-power game, and that the proper war aim should be the replacement of existing militarist kingdoms with democratic units delimited by community of language, religion and habit — 'grouped in federations of United States when their extent makes them politically unwieldy'.

All this was good sense in 1914, just as it is today. But the British public had had its attention focused for it on certain simplistic views of the war situation, with Britain cast in the role of chivalrous defender of the rights of small nations (a view that caused much ironic amusement amongst intelligent Irishmen), and was not prepared, with a war on its hands, to [122] enter philosophic debate about the correctness of these views. The British popular press had only to accuse the author of *Commonsense* of being on the side of the Huns for him to become, like Ibsen's Dr Stockmann, an enemy of the people.

Shaw might have had his windows broken, like his fellow-Dubliner the Duke of Wellington during the reform crisis, if the sensation-mongers hadn't overdone things and created a reaction. The public, not being the utter fools that newspaper editors and political party strategists often take them to be, tend to get uneasy about virulent newspaper campaigns against individuals. True, some of Shaw's friends took sides against him, astonishing him by their resentment which, he concluded, they must have been concealing for many years. When he appeared at public functions there were those who pointedly got up and left. But most remained, and when people had time to think things over they felt there was something to be said for his viewpoint after all, intemperately expressed though it might be. Shaw for his part didn't keep a low profile. He returned to the attack with a follow-up pamphlet, but the editor of the *New Statesman*, Clifford Sharp, another hidden foe, refused to publish it. Shaw swallowed the insult, as he did many others from the same person, the result being yet another reaction in his favour and a growing conviction that the editor of the *New Statesman* had been gratuitously offensive to a distinguished author. Clifford Sharp finally got so big for his boots that he left the *New Statesman*, found to his surprise that he wasn't snapped up by other papers and ended up cadging for book reviews around Fleet Street.

Shaw remained prominent in the public arena, often seriously distracting attention from the war, as he said himself. He contributed to a volume published by the Humanitarian League, *Killing for Sport*, then as now a sore subject. Meanwhile Charlotte, who had taken the Mrs Pat episode very badly, had recovered sufficiently to bring out an English version of *Damaged Goods* by the French playwright Eugene Brieux, hailed by Shaw as the modern Sophocles. She provided it with a preface which showed that sixteen years of living with Shaw had caused her to write astonishingly like him.

The year 1916 brought him into unfavourable prominence yet again. The Dublin Rising on Easter Monday, in which telegraphic communication with Britain was interrupted, was at first only scrappily reported by Fleet Street. By the time communications were restored the military authorities, who had taken charge of Dublin, were vying in unintelligence with the Corporation in their handling of awkward situations. They assumed that the wave of anti-insurgent feeling in Dublin immediately after the Rising gave them *carte blanche* to apply a military solution – *their* kind of military solution – to a political problem. Accordingly they held secret courts martial, condemned the insurgent leaders to death and shot them. The announcement of the executions was the first the public knew of what was happening, a consideration which didn't stop certain British newspapers from bragging that no one in Ireland had petitioned for the insurgents' lives to be spared.

Britain for its part remained furious with Ireland, deeming the Rising to be the meanest kind of stab in the back, particularly since home rule had been enacted and was to come into effect after the war. Shaw, living in the midst of the raging Britons, braved their rage by pointing out in a letter to the *Daily News* (10 May 1916) that the men shot in cold blood after surrendering were prisoners of war, so that Britain was 'entirely incorrect' in slaughtering them. Two days later two more insurgents were shot, James Connolly, whose leg had been shattered in the fighting, being brought by ambulance from his infirmary bed and propped in a chair in order to be done to death.

This was the last straw for everyone. The prime minister, Asquith, whose son had wanted Shaw shot for writing *Commonsense*, crossed to Dublin, delivered himself of several Broadbentic utterances, visited a hospital and effusively shook so many hands that he managed to greet several rebels before he could be stopped. On his return to Downing Street he announced that negotiations for an Irish peace would be entrusted to that zealous Celt Lloyd George who, when not in the arms of any of his numerous mistresses, was solving the nation's problems at a rate of knots.

Yeats, like Shaw, was in London amongst the raging Britons at this time. But no public word about his savaged country or his slaughtered compatriots escaped his lips. He drafted a poem, 'Easter 1916', and, several weeks *after* the executions had the poem printed in an edition of twenty-five copies for circulation among friends.

Nor was he more outspoken when Roger Casement was caught and tried for his life. But once again Shaw came forward to do what he could to save the doomed man, drafting a defence which took the ground that Casement was not a detected traitor but a prisoner of war and, as such, entitled to his life. Casement preferred the futile legalistic defence put up by Serjeant Sullivan, coincidentally a tenant of Charlotte's old home in Rosscarbery, and apparently so tricky that Charlotte expressed regret at having anything to do with him. When sentenced to hang, Casement made a Robert Emmet-type speech from the dock and converted, in the con- demned cell, from Ulster Protestantism to Roman Catholicism. Shaw drafted a petition for his reprieve, but remained in the background. He refrained from signing the petition in case this would frighten off more influential signatories, although he knew that the absence of his signature would expose him to taunts of moral cowardice. Shaw, like many other public men at that time, had been informed of the existence of the notorious diaries, but ignored them as irrelevant.

Subsequent events proved Shaw right about Casement and the diaries, as did his prophecy in *Peace Conference Hints* (1919) that the next war would feature scientific attempts to destroy cities and kill citizens, leaving the military comparatively safe in their dugouts. He had been disappointed in his hope of being made a member of the Irish Convention (1917), one of the long line of ad hoc deliberative bodies set up to solve the Irish problem. His hope for a seat in the Convention shows the persistence of his ambition to play an important part in public administration, towards which his vestry seat had been intended as a first step. He had reproached Shakespeare for being merely the ablest playwright of his time instead of its ablest statesman. The urge to rule was in Shaw's blood as well as in his nature, his Shavian forebears having taken to parliament and to the judicial bench like ducks to water. He must have envied Webb for being appointed Secretary of State for the Colonies (the department in which Webb was once a resident clerk), although he would probably have accepted the leadership of any public body which offered him the chance to exercise his administrative ability.

No inspired prime minister being at hand to offer

him that chance, Shaw was left to be only his age's ablest playwright. But from *Heartbreak House* (1919) onwards he played out his role of statesman through his dramatic puppets, his themes being chiefly political and public in their nature rather than personal and private. Monarchs, prime ministers, governors of all kinds become his central characters. *The Apple Cart* (1928) is frankly a dramatised cabinet meeting, with a sex scherzando as interlude to amuse the ladies; and *Geneva* (1938) brings Europe's dictators on the stage in a curious anticipation of those 'summit conferences' of our own time, except that Shaw's speeches for Herr Battler, Signor Bombardone, Commissar Posky and General Flanco de Fortinbras have at least the merit of being intelligible and entertaining.

One small consolation prize did fall to him. Early in 1917 the British commander-in-chief, Haig, invited Shaw to visit him at the front. The idea was that Shaw would then write an account of what he saw — or was let see — and would keep up the spirits of those at home by assuring them that Haig was doing a really fine job. Which is more or less what Shaw did, as did the other prominent authors and journalists who were brought out for the same purpose. The odd thing is that Shaw seems to have been taken in by this bit of Haigery.

7

The war years made it a thin time for serious theatre, leaving the serious playwright with little incentive to write. Shaw therefore took his time over *Heartbreak House* and occupied himself in other directions. He gave a lot of attention to the cinema, the possibilities of which he had perceived as early as 1908. In a letter to Pinero that year he mentioned that the developing cinema seemed to offer them both a chance of a new career. In 1914 he took part in a silent fun movie, a skit about cowboys. The other stars, all togged out as cowboys and toting their guns in closed holsters obviously borrowed from army officers, included William Archer and G. K. Chesterton, and the director was J. M. Barrie. The following year, when *Great Catherine* was published, Shaw claimed that it would make an excellent movie, and in the autumn of 1916 was letting it be known that if he did decide to 'meddle with the cinema theatre' it would be by writing specially for it.

For convenience we can deal at this point with his filmed plays. After some minor and unsuccessful forays into the cinema during the 1920s, he got his first real chance of cinema success with the establishment of the talkies. He had irritably rejected offers of large sums for his film rights during the silent era, knowing that it was not his texts the moguls were after but the use of his name. A Shaw play without the dialogue was about as useful as a Beethoven symphony without the notes. The talkies changed the situation: dialogue became a practical proposition. Again, it was the Germans who were first in the field although their *Pygmalion* (1935) departed so much from the sacred scripture that Shaw was furious. The next filmed *Pygmalion* was a Dutch version, just as much a travesty as the German, and just as little pleasing to the author. He was to be third time lucky with the British version, produced by Gabriel Pascal.

Pascal (not his real name) was a Hungarian adventurer who appeared from nowhere on Shaw's doorstep, without capital, without backers, without any tally of provable achievement in the film world though with large claims in his direction, for he was a fluent and imaginative liar. Shaw of course saw through the boasting and the lying and would have accepted that Pascal's name should be spelt with an [128] R, not a P. But he also saw the artist in Pascal; he liked the daring and the imaginativeness and noted the similarity to the lately deceased Frank Harris. Vandeleur Lee had early accustomed him to the type, and he knew its uses. Above all he liked what Pascal was offering. This was to film *Pygmalion* in strict accordance with the author's wishes. Pascal gave him five days to think the matter over, saying he would go on his way if he had not been awarded the film rights by four o'clock on the afternoon of the following Friday.

Blanche Patch tells us in her *30 Years with G. B. S.* that Shaw left Pascal in suspense until precisely four o'clock, when a special messenger arrived at his flat in Duke Street, just as Pascal was packing his bag, and placed the required document in his hand. (This is suspected to have been yet another Pascal invention but Blanche Patch, in conversation with the author, insisted that it was quite true.)

With the rights in his possession, Pascal had little trouble in raising the needed capital and getting his show on the road. But he didn't keep his word about strictly observing the author's wishes. Shaw was delighted to have Wendy Hiller play Eliza but wasn't allowed to have Charles Laughton, plump middle-aged, magnetic, and a character actor of genius, as Higgins. But the film, with Leslie Howard (another Hungarian) as Higgins, and with the skilled Anthony Asquith as director, won the hearts of the critics as well as audiences by its unobtrusive insistence that, no matter what the author might say, Eliza and Higgins would somehow end up in each other's arms.

This version of *Pygmalion* gained an Oscar for Shaw who, according to Blanche Patch, remained for a long time under the impression that the award was named after Wilde.*

*Communicated in conversation with the author.

Pascal was now authorised to tackle *Major Barbara*. It was his curious belief that this was Shaw's 'most universal' play. But Wendy Hiller, a superb and touching Eliza, proved a wooden and lack lustre Barbara and Rex Harrison not the ideal Cusins. The *Pygmalion* success was not repeated. Shaw, however, was still prepared to allow Pascal to try his hand with *Caesar and Cleopatra*. J. Arthur Rank, who like Shaw's father was in corn and flour, put up the money for what was to be an epic in full colour, and found that Pascal spent it on a truly epic scale. Pascal not only cured the flour merchant of any desire to have dealings with him ever again but antagonised his stars (Vivien Leigh and Claude Rains) and his film crews by displays of arrogance, ill temper and inefficiency. When the film was at last in the can the technicians, through their union, passed a resolution which virtually 'blacked' Pascal.

Caesar and Cleopatra, in spite of the exquisite Vivien Leigh and of Stewart Grainger in the full bloom of his women's mag good looks, failed to sweep the world. There were several fine individual performances but the film as a whole, which had been directed as well as produced by Pascal, was too ponderous to be popular. Moreover, it came before the public in December 1945, a time when the memories of what dictators can do were too fresh to allow much liking for Caesars, even for one so benign as Shaw's.

The shortcomings of *Caesar and Cleopatra* gravely damaged the Pascal mystique, but so long as Pascal remained the only person to whom Shaw would entrust his English language film rights he had to be put up with. Backers were still available in encouraging numbers for it was believed that another *Pygmalion* success was possible so long as Pascal could be kept from actually directing it. But Shaw's contract required Pascal to direct and not to share responsibility with anyone else. Ways and means of getting around this provision were canvassed, and various proposals were made for more productions, but in the heel of the hunt Pascal was obliged to turn his attention to Italy and to Ireland for finance and for production facilities. The bait for Ireland was *Saint Joan*, Shaw providing background support for Pascal by successfully arousing Eamon de Valera's interest in the prospects of the Irish film industry. Joe McGrath, former freedom fighter, former Minister for Industry and Commerce in a Cosgrave adminis- tration, and now Hospitals Sweepstakes millionaire, appeared willing to put up a five-figure sum to help establish an Irish film making company, the govern- ment promising to come in later on with money raised by a tariff on imported films. Another former freedom fighter, Dan Breen, declared himself willing to invest, likewise the influential solicitor Arthur Cox.

But Irish Screen Arts Ltd, as that company was called, could raise only £41,000 when a quarter of a million was required, for Joe McGrath's enthusiasm had waned. This was perhaps because he had been belatedly informed of Rank's sufferings with Pascal, perhaps because Cox's sensitive Catholic antennae had picked up the rumour that Pope Pius XII's advisers were not happy about having their Church's burning of a saint sympathetically explained and defended to cinema audiences by an Irish lapsed Protestant.

This was the end of the trail for Pascal. Other men were to make Shaw films when Shaw was no longer alive and able to defend the integrity of his texts, but only one film, *The Doctor's Dilemma*, directed by Anthony Asquith, had any real merit.

5
The Grand Old Man

1

Shaw had asked to be appointed a member of the 1917 Irish Convention and made no secret of this. There was no mock modesty about his first reason: that he was a pre-eminent celebrity. His other reason was that he had worked out how the British-Irish problem could be solved for once and for all. This was not through separation and independence for Ireland (with part of Ulster excluded), but home rule for each of the constituent races under a federal parliament. But since the Irish Convention was intended to be a way of getting the Northern and Southern Irish leaders to talk themselves out of their differences, it seemed pointless to the British to throw amongst the cats a pigeon who wanted to plan a complete reorganisation of the British Isles at a moment when it seemed those Isles might be conquered by the Germans.

Shaw was therefore not made a member and Sir Horace Plunkett, high priest of the co-operative movement, was.

Shaw, denied a direct voice in the Convention, tried to play the old Fabian trick of permeation. He rightly believed that he could manipulate Plunkett, who was chairman of the Convention, because everyone else could do so. Plunkett was one of those intelligent, well-meaning persons who deal with a famine by throwing themselves into the task of getting out a report on the most efficient way to distribute the food which isn't there. Shaw drafted a Convention report for Plunkett, but he had merely wasted his time, for the Convention came to an end without the Northern and Southern representatives finding any common ground. Besides, the emergence of Sinn Féin as a power in the South was quickening the expectations of radical nationalists. The fact that 'moderate' home rulers could not find agreement with the North confirmed the British government in its original cynicism towards the Convention; it simply ignored the Convention's report.

O'Flaherty, V.C., a playlet written to help the recruiting drive, although hilariously accurate in its observation of Irish country life, is unlikely to have drawn many Irishmen to the colours whose own adventurousness or necessity hadn't already disposed them to join up. In September 1918 the writer Stephen Gwynn, then a captain in the army, got in touch with Shaw who was on holiday in Parknasilla. He asked for more assistance for the recruiting campaign. Shaw responded with a substantial 'open letter' to Colonel Lynch, M.P., much in the style of the *Drapier's Letters*. Publication was entrusted to the Dublin firm, Maunsel & Co., and the proofs didn't reach Shaw until October. By then events had caught up with him and he was obliged to provide his open letter with a foreword explaining that although the German empire had crumbled it was still necessary for Irishmen to join up as a point of honour. Shaw dated his foreword for the day Maunsel & Co. said they would publish. That was to be 10 November 1918.

The following day the war stopped, and the booklet, entitled *War Issues for Irishmen*, was scrapped except for a few copies.

Heartbreak House, finished in 1917 after an unusually prolonged gestation and written while Shaw was willingly under the spell of Chekhov, was regarded by some as his masterpiece. This was his own opinion, at least for a time. Blanche Patch reports that witnessing any Chekhov play caused him to exclaim that he wanted to go home and burn all his own. Nevertheless, he was also given to hinting broadly that comparisons might be drawn between the central character of *Heartbreak House*, Captain Shotover, aged father of two daughters, and Shakespeare's tragic father of three. Finally, in his little piece for puppets, *Shakes versus Shav*, he unambiguously claims to have created a rival Lear.

Heartbreak House, a farewell to leisured, cultured Europe before World War I, earnestly warns us that unless we plot our political voyage more intelligently than we do, we will end up on the rocks. *On the Rocks* was in fact to be the title of a later play. *Heartbreak House* failed on its first production, allegedly because of bad casting. The failure depressed the author uncharacteristically, experienced as he was in rebuffs. He later admitted that during his sixties he felt he was fading, which in a way he was, though only by the standards of his younger self. By comparison with other sexagenarians he was remarkably spry both in body and in mind, and his next work for the theatre was *Back to Methusaleh*, a kind of monumental dramatic symphony in five movements. The time-span ranges from the Garden of Eden to as far as thought can reach, the characters from Adam and Eve to the future race of Ancients, the Life Force's virtually incorporeal agents for pure thought. *Back to Methusaleh*, which Shaw offers as a new Bible for the modern world, argues that mankind's salvation lies in willing itself to extend the normal lifespan of three score years and ten to three centuries, for it will take us this length of time to grow out of our childish follies and wickednesses, our preoccupation with gratifying our senses, even our pleasure in the fine arts, and to become vessels of pure thought in the service of the Life Force.

The characters of *Back to Methusaleh* include brilliant sketches of two prime ministers, Asquith and Lloyd George (Lubin and Burge), who reappear in future times as the prime minister Burge-Lubin and enjoy yet another reincarnation as the Envoy Badger Bluebin who, like all politicians, resembles an imperfectly reformed criminal disguised by a good tailor.

Back to Methusaleh, written for an as yet non-existent dramatic Bayreuth, was, to the author's astonishment, produced by Barry Jackson at the Birmingham Repertory Theatre, where it was received with one of those great emotional outbursts in which mankind can chivalrously express its admiration for what it conceives to be a great feat. This *Back to Methusaleh* unquestionably is, its only rival being Ibsen's *Emperor and Galilean*. But its length prevents its becoming popular (it needs at least three evenings to be performed in its entirety), although the current tendency in television is towards multi-instalment dramas and a complete *Back to Methusaleh* on the small screen would therefore be quite in the fashion. The average person however does not find attractive the Utopia proposed by Shaw: so complete a triumph of mind over matter that there is no bodily matter left at all.

The next play by our fading sexagenarian was one which conquered the theatre world as no other play has done since Shakespeare. *Saint Joan* (1923) had almost the effect of extending Joan's sanctified status to the author.

Joan of Arc was canonised in 1920. Shaw's friend Sydney Cockerell, curator of the Fitzwilliam Museum at Cambridge, suggested to him that the new saint would make a good subject for a play. Shaw agreed, for he was always on the lookout for a striking woman character. But he did not take fire at the idea, and it was left to Charlotte to get to work on him. Books and articles about Joan were left lying around the house, apparently by accident, where Shaw was sure to come across them. The ruse worked. In April 1923 he started *Saint Joan* and finished it in four months, much of it being written while he was in Co. Kerry. The saint is presented to us as one of the first Protestant martyrs: Protestant because she places the promptings of conscience above the authority of the Catholic Church. Shaw also makes her one of the early apostles of nationalism, a Napoleonic realist in warfare and a pioneer of rational dress for women.

Since his plays were panned as a matter of course when first produced in London, he had adopted the practice of introducing them either in Germany or in Vienna, where they usually enjoyed a good reception. (He was extremely well served by his German translator, Siegfried Trebitsch.) In the case of *Saint Joan* it was first published in a German translation and first staged in New York, but did not really take off until Sybil Thorndike played Joan in London under the author's guidance. After that the play simply went around the world and the title role became for actresses what Hamlet is for actors.

Man and Superman had made him famous, *Pygmalion* made him popular, *Saint Joan* made him respected and raised him to acknowledged classic status. The Nobel Prize, awarded to Yeats in 1923,

could hardly be withheld from him any longer. He
got it in 1925, presumably, he said, in recognition
of his having written nothing that year. He accepted
the honour without elation, remarking that it was a
lottery which anyone with a certain minimum of
celebrity could win, and devoted his prize money to
establishing a fund for promoting in England a knowledge of Swedish literature and culture.

In 1926 he became seventy and was officially
congratulated by the German government; the British
government, as he remarked, merely prohibited the
broadcasting of any words spoken by him on his
birthday. Naturally he rose to the occasion. In his
birthday speech the new septuagenarian declared that
he did not care a snap of the fingers for his literary
eminence in comparison with his pioneering and con-
structive work as one of the founders of the British
Labour Party.

The government of his native land extended to
him the charity of its silence.

3

Five years elapsed between the writing of *Saint Joan*
and the appearance of *The Applecart*. These had been
largely spent in compiling his *Intelligent Woman's
Guide to Socialism and Capitalism*. The impulse to
write this had been provided by his sister-in-law Cissy
Cholmondeley who had asked him for a leaflet she
could use to explain socialism to the local Women's
Institute. Poor Sissy got far more than she bargained
for: a treatise whose 200,000 words would have
taken her a long time to read to the ladies of the
village of Wem. Ramsay MacDonald, soaring to
heights of humbug rarely attained even by that
master, proclaimed the *Guide* humanity's most important book after the Bible, and it has indeed resembled

the Bible in being more reverenced than read.

The *Guide* is a fair exposition of the various polit- ical creeds being preached at the period, and hammers the point home that unless socialism means equality of income for all, and that income guaranteed, it means nothing. Ten years later, in view of the development of other political creeds in the meantime (fascism, national socialism, and so on), he published *Everybody's Political What's What?* which covered a lot of the ground already gone over in the *Guide* and proved another very laboursome work. Neither, however, is in the least laboursome to read, and both remain high on the list of books to be read by the young who are anxious to find their bearings.

The Applecart proved as successful in its way as *Saint Joan*. The immediate occasion for writing it was Barry Jackson's proposal to inaugurate a festival of Shaw's plays to be held every year at Malvern. Shaw realised that the best send-off the new festival could have was a new play and, while staying with Lord and Lady Astor, who ran a species of perpetual political summer school at their stately home, Cliveden, wrote it during the last seven weeks of 1928. So the play opens with a conversation between Buckingham Palace officials about people who are more impressed by symbols than by the realities symbolised, and only then gets down to its main business of demonstrating how a popular monarch can outsmart his cabinet, who want to gag him, by threatening to abdicate and, having dissolved parliament, standing for election himself and forming his own party.

At this, the cabinet capitulates and drops the threat to gag their monarch.

The critics rashly jumped to the conclusion that in *The Applecart* Shaw had abandoned his lifelong republican principles and turned monarchist. But he was only too happy to set them right in the preface to the published text.

The Applecart was the last of his major successes. The plays continued to come from him and continued to be very notable works of dramatic art. But Noel Coward and others of that school had, by their mastery of the crisp crackling style, made their kind of play the only fashionable wear for the time. Beside them Shaw seemed wordy and laboured, and his habit of hammering home his points and his jokes was turning into a very noticeable fault. Like Bach, he delighted in exhaustive expression and in stuffing his work with counterpoint. Chesterton, a discerning admirer and an acute critic, had pointed to this tendency years before, reminding Shaw that when one feels obliged to define every word in one's own special terms and to cover every contingency, then the argument moves but slowly.

Again, the plays which followed *The Applecart* were too political and too sociological for the taste of the times and in spite of the author's skill and ingenuity in sugaring pills can have made little appeal to women, whose tastes remain decisive in the theatre. The early 1930s, being a period of dire economic depression, set up a fashion for escapism in the theatre, to which the rubbing in of harsh realities in *Too True to be Good, On the Rocks*, and *The Simpleton of the Unexpected Isles* proved uncongenial. Besides, Shaw was returning to the mood in which he had written *Back to Methusaleh*. He was deliberately disregarding the requirements, even the possibilities of the commercial theatre of those times, with a recklessness he had never before allowed himself. Perhaps he felt, like Beethoven with his late quartets, that these plays would have their day some time, and in this he may not have been altogether wrong. They continue to have their staunch champions, the free and colourful fantasy of *The Simpleton* being now quite in fashion, and the [139] depressed political conditions in which they were written have repeated themselves in the 'recessionary' 1980s.

We encounter too in these plays an unaccustomed note of despair, a harping on the dangers ahead. His household was also beginning to notice signs in him of unwonted irritability. The fact is, he was beginning to die from pernicious anaemia, the disease which had killed his venerated Samuel Butler thirty-five years before. Shaw might well have joined Butler by 1939 or thereabouts if a distinguished pathologist, Dr Geoffrey Evans (1886-1951) had not diagnosed the trouble and arrested its progress with massive doses of liver extract, injected without its being made altogether clear to the aged vegetarian what he was getting. Since Shaw started perking up again his claims for the total sufficiency of a vegetarian diet are open to doubt.

4

In 1931 Shaw acted on a suggestion that he should visit Russia and see for himself something of the world's first large-scale practice of socialism. For some reason or other Charlotte didn't go on this journey, so Shaw's companions were Lord and Lady Astor and Lord Lothian. It may be that Charlotte asked Lady Astor to take special care of Shaw, though it is more likely that Lady Astor appointed herself his nursemaid without anyone's by-your-leave, least of all Shaw's. That she was a conscientious nursemaid is beyond question. She was observed in her charge's hotel bedroom in Moscow, personally shampooing his hair.

The visitors had a long interview with Stalin, whom

Lady Astor hectored and Shaw found genial, hand- some and humorous. At the end of the year he was off again, this time to South Africa with Charlotte. They brought their car and chauffeur but Shaw insisted on doing much of the driving, declining to accept that at seventy-six his reactions were not as quick as they once had been. He steered off the road, pressed the accelerator instead of the brake and bumped so much over the veldt that poor Charlotte, in the back seat, got such a bad shaking that she had to spend several weeks in hospital. Her first question on being lifted out of the car was about Shaw's safety. He had escaped unhurt.

But not even driving accidents, let alone holidays or travelling, were allowed to intefere with his work routine. Every morning had to produce its tale of words in his meticulously formed shorthand, the sheets being posted to his secretary in London to be transcribed, more or less accurately, on her type- writer. So while Charlotte was in hospital he occupied himself by writing *The Adventures of the Black Girl in her Search for God.*

The Black Girl, a survey of the differing views of God presented in the Bible, and of the teachings of Jesus and of Mahomet, shocked the conventionally pious, partly because of the freedom with which Jesus and his doctrines were discussed (he was regarded just as one of several great teachers of mankind), partly because of the striking illustrations provided by John Farleigh, which showed the Black Girl nude even in Jesus's presence. The book sold well, over 200,000 copies, but the equating of Jesus's miracles with conjuring tricks, not to mention the nudity, was enough to have the book banned in some of Britain's public libraries and of course in Ireland. In Ireland the repercussions were felt not alone in the traditionally sensitive areas but in the Co. Wexford

Bee Keepers Association of which, through owning a small ancestral property in Wexford, Shaw was a life member. The association found itself faced with a motion that he be expelled. It is pleasing to be able to report that the beekeepers at their annual meeting dismissed the motion with dignified contempt.

The following year Shaw and Charlotte took another long winter cruise, during the first month of which (January 1933) he wrote *Village Wooing*, a short piece for two players on his favourite theme of the pursuit of the male by the female. It must surely be one of the most charming works of its kind, his *Eine Kleine Nachtmusik* so to speak. During this cruise he set foot on American soil for the first and last time. From the moment it had become known that the cruise would take him to America he was pestered with invitations to address all kinds of bodies. Seduced by the imposing title of The Academy of Political Science, which seemed to identify it as 'the most important body in America today' (his own words), he agreed to address it in New York. The Met Opera House was booked out for the occasion. Unfortunately the Academy of Political Science bore about the same relation to an academy of political science as Frank Harris's *Life and Loves* to St Augustine's *Confessions*, and felt badly about being given a lecture on political science instead of a series of comic turns by a well-known funny man. The lecture was later published as *The Political Madhouse in America and Nearer Home*.

In 1935 he managed to knock into some kind of presentability a play which had given him an unusual amount of trouble, *The Millionairess*. The lady in question, who inherits her millions from a remarkable father, is Shaw's female Caesar. For this character he drew on Beatrice Webb's real-life experience of sweated labour (which Beatrice had undergone for research purposes), although most of his lady Caeser's characteristics seem to have been taken from Lady Astor. At this period he was publicly reverenced by men like Desmond MacCarthy as a great teacher of mankind, called by James Agate 'the greatest living Englishman' (!) and in Winston Churchill's *Great Contemporaries* 'the greatest living master of letters in the English-speaking world'. Nevertheless the West End theatre managers continued not to beat a path to his door. The first British performance of *The Millionairess* was not in Shaftesbury Avenue but in Bexhill.

For the 1939 Malvern Festival he provided his last great dramatic work, *In Good King Charles's Golden Days*, the only play about Charles II, he boasted, that was not about Nell Gwynn. Nell does in fact appear in it, a genial, able and charming woman who makes a favourable contrast with the beautiful but termagent Lady Castlemaine. (They are virtually Blanche and Julia of *The Philanderer* in Caroline costume.) The chief interest of the play is in the bringing together for an imaginary conversation of half a dozen late seventeenth-century notables: Isaac Newton, George Fox, Godfrey Kneller, Charles himself as the intelligent pragmatist, and his brother, the future James II, as the obstinate believer in the divine right of kings. I own to a little disappointment that we are given the man of science, the man of religion, the painter and the statesman, but not Henry Purcell, the musician, to be the mouthpiece for Shaw's views upon the finest of the fine arts.

The play ends with a glimpse of Charles as husband. Speaking as the pursuer and the pursued of many women, he stresses how he has in fact remained faithful to his wife, his extra-marital adventures being no more than biological responses to biological urges. Queen Catherine, playing Charlotte to Charles's

Shaw, obligingly ignores any question of the woman's right to respond to *her* biological urges. She merely admits that she experienced only one bout of jealousy (over the Duchess of Richmond) much as Charlotte had been shaken by the Mrs Pat Campbell episode. She reassures her consort that the other women, 'the servants of your common pleasures', have left her free to be 'something more to you than they are or ever can be'. Her Charlottesque conclusion, mutually comforting, is to agree that 'you have never been really unfaithful to me'. Clearly the scene, though a justified and relevant part of the play, which makes a touching and effective closing scene, is intended to be a bouquet to Charlotte, the conferring upon her of the Order of Matrimonial Merit, and an apologia for Shaw's own love life.

The tribute was timely. Charlotte was beginning to suffer from what was at first thought to be bad rheumatism or arthritis but turned out to be *osteitis deformans*. It made increasingly miserable her last four years of life.

5

World War II began in September 1939 in spite of Shaw's vigorous efforts to stop it by personal command. He had deemed it beyond mankind's remarkable capacity for folly for the nations to blow up each other cities. He opposed Ireland's neutrality, declaring that it would make the invasion of Ireland inevitable, that little country not having the resources of population or military muscle needed for effective resistance. When the 'phoney war' ended in 1940 and the belligerents got down to real business, Irish neutrality became a very urgent problem for Britain. Shaw offended and frightened his fellow-countrymen by endorsing Britain's right to resume control of certain Irish ports. He told de Valera that in this international crisis the ports did not belong to Ireland but 'to Europe, to the world, to civilisation, to the Most Holy Trinity as you might say, and are only held in trust by your Government in Dublin. In their name we must borrow the ports from you for the duration.'

In the event, de Valera got away with his neutrality. Britain hesitated to seize the Southern ports for fear of offending American-Irish opinion, ever influential in the United States and always more Irish than native Irish opinion. Britain contented herself with the Northern ports and, on America's entry into the conflict, with the use of Northern Ireland as an American base. Thus, as Shaw dryly pointed out, de Valera's neutrality was preserved by the partition he abhorred.

In 1943 Charlotte, who had been dying by inches, rather suddenly completed the process in the early hours of Sunday 12 September in their London flat in Whitehall Court. The nurses, in round-the-clock attendance upon her, did not inform Shaw until he was awakened at his accustomed hour. On hastening into her room he found her looking, as the newly dead so often do, younger and handsomer than in her last days. But the comforting illusion did not last long. Before the day was out she again looked the old, worn out, crippled woman. Outwardly he bore her departure with calm, later that morning asking a business caller if any change were noticeable in him. On being told No, he remarked with a show of unconcern that he had been a widower since 2.30 a.m. He thus adroitly maintained his legendary character and obtained the solitude he required at this terrible time, for the disconcerted caller escaped as quickly as possible. Shaw was to emphasise the relief her death had been, for towards the end her mind as well

as her body was afflicted, and she had imagined that
the flat was filled with strangers. He said that one
more year of her illness would have killed him. But
all during the first day of widowerhood he kept
going in and out of her room to talk to the lifeless
shape on the bed. By degrees he was adapting himself
to the realisation that he was now quite alone, the
last survivor of the clan, for the hordes of Gurly
relations were nothing to him, a couple of honourable self-reliants excepted, save as importuning
nuisances; and his Shaw connections, still reverently
satelliting around the family baronet, retained their
preposterous stand-offishness.

Charlotte's death was characteristically unobtrusive.
Unlike his sister Lucy's a quarter of a century before,
it defied artistic treatment by his pen. One March
afternoon in 1920, before he was quite over a dis-
abling dose of influenza, he had gone to visit the
ailing Lucy:

> When I had sat with her a little while she said:
> "I am dying." I took her hand to encourage her
> and said, rather conventionally, "Oh no: you will
> be all right presently." We were silent then; and
> there was no sound except from somebody playing
> the piano in the nearest house (it was a fine even-
> ing and all the windows were open) until there
> was a very faint flutter in her throat. She was still
> holding my hand. Then her thumb straightened.
> She was dead. (*Sixteen Self Sketches*, p. 95)

Charlotte, like Lucy and his mother, was cremated.
In the case of his sister and his mother he had been
able to go into the furnace room and see them burn,
noting that Lucy burnt with a steady white light
like that of a wax candle, coal being scarce in 1920.
He could not tell us how Charlotte burned. By 1943
mourners were no longer allowed into the furnace

room. We only know that Charlotte departed from mortal view to the music of Handel, which she had loved. She had told some friends that she wanted her ashes scattered on a Dublin hill known as the Three Rock Mountain. But Shaw instructed the crematorium authorities to retain them until they could be mingled with his own.

Apart from some minor legacies, including £1,000 to Sidney Webb (who too was a recent widower), Charlotte left her money (over £100,000) to Shaw for his life. Thereafter it was to finance a scheme to decorate the Irish with an appearance of *savoir faire* by bringing some of the masterpieces of fine art within their reach. The project was ungraciously summarised by the intended beneficiaries as an attempt to civilise Irishmen by a woman who knew the need for it, having been married to one for forty-five years. The project proved of small use, partly because good samaritanship in this area requires far more money than Charlotte's legacy provided, partly because inflation soon made that little less.

6

Seven years of life remained to him. In 1944 he published *Everybody's Political What's What?* which is precisely what the title says it is. It is full of good things, expressed with vigour and with clarity, and all in all an astonishing achievement for a man of eighty-eight. As already related, he devoted much time and energy at this period to the filming of his plays. Collected editions of his work had been issued in the early 1930s and after the war he issued another edition, the Standard, though this was to be superseded thirty-five years later by the magnificently complete edition supervised by Dan H. Laurence, unquestionably the first Shaw scholar of the day.

In 1946 he reached ninety, and *Picture Post* expressed in a birthday tribute the feelings of many:

> The proper attitude for us is gratitude — to a fellow man for a life of incessant painstaking and devoted work — devoted to our enlightenment.

Certain of Shaw's fellow Dubliners could not subscribe to this view. The proposal that Dublin Corporation bestow upon him the freedom of the city enabled some city fathers to display their sense of occasion. Their unmannerly sniping did not wound him. Rather did he welcome the opportunity, rare in his period of worldwide acclaim, to show he was still able to deal with humbugs. A city father who pronounced him no fit mentor for the youth or the adults of Ireland was felled with two words: 'Who is?'

An alderman, later to be a Lord Mayor of Dublin, brayed that Shaw's 'intellectualism' had brought the world to the sad state it was then in, that it was an intellectualism which scoffed at revealed religion, even at the very existence of God, and moreover was in conflict with the intellectualism of St Thomas Aquinas. Shaw used a more humane killer for the alderman than others might have done. I had some acquaintance with this alderman and would declare him extremely unlikely ever to have read a line of Aquinas in his life or to have been able to grasp its meaning if he had. But his fellow councillors, antagonised by having brandished in their faces such exotica as 'intellectualism' and 'Aquinas', gave the alderman a lesson in municipal democracy by voting Shaw the freedom.

He accepted, thanking Jim Larkin for his efforts in the matter and mentioning that his father had been a hereditary freeman. He begged to be excused from making the journey to Dublin, evaded an offer to have the entire Corporation make the journey to him, and settled for a small deputation to Ayot headed by the city manager and the Irish High Commissioner, John Dulanty.

I believe he would have preferred not to have been offered the freedom of a city he despised, and accepted it only because it would have been too ungracious to refuse. He was clearly better pleased by the spontaneous birthday gift of a Dublin dustman named O'Reilly, who sent him a tiny gold shamrock. He attached the trinket to his watchchain, telling O'Reilly that there it would remain until he himself fell off it. O'Reilly was also the onlie begetter of the scheme to affix a gigantic plaque (about the size of a dustbin lid) to Shaw's birthplace. Mr O'Reilly failed to collect enough donations from Dubliners to defray the cost, and refused offers from abroad to settle the debt, wishing it to stand as a reproach to the city. In conversation with Mr O'Reilly I learned that his knowledge of Shaw's work derived solely from witnessing the *Pygmalion* film. The portrayal of Dustman Doolittle as an intelligent man and an original moralist convinced him that Shaw was truly the twentieth-century Shakespeare (another instinctive judgment, for he had not got around to reading the Bard), and was therefore worthy of the gratitude and honour of the dustman fraternity. To many Dubliners, Mr O'Reilly was a figure of fun, and was even sneered at to his face. Such treatment did not discompose him in the least. 'You have to be a Bernard Shaw,' he said, 'to realise that dustmen have minds like everybody else.'

Not, I imagine, the least handsome tribute to Shaw at ninety.

He continued to write, to take a perky interest in affairs, to deal with overwhelming correspondence, and to hold his own in controversy with much of the old ingenuity. His *Sixteen Self Sketches*, an unusually slender volume for him, was mostly a gathering of pieces written long before. *Buoyant Billions* and *Farfetched Fables* are gallant efforts to draw again the bow of Ulysses, and the very last play of all, completed just before his 94th birthday, was the miniature *Why She Would Not*, written, he admitted, because now that he had said all he wanted to say he felt entitled to write little things to amuse himself.

After Charlotte's death he had exchanged their relatively spacious flat in Whitehall Court for a smaller one, chiefly for Blanche Patch to use as an office. He seldom went to London, preferring to stay at the house in Ayot he and Charlotte had rented as a temporary measure in 1906 and had finally bought as the alternative to having to move. With no Charlotte to drag him away on foreign tours, his travellings were confined to occasional afternoon drives around the Hertfordshire lanes in the Rolls-Royce which, like the old man's mistress, was more for display than use. He was fond of saying that, left to himself, he would have lived and died in the same house he was born in.

One old habit he did keep up: corresponding with actresses. One of them, the American Molly Tompkins, wanted to move in on him after Charlotte's death when he had rather incautiously boasted of being the world's most eligible bachelor. Molly was warned off quite brusquely. Nevertheless he continued to have a soft spot for her, possibly because of an encounter they had in Italy when he was seventy and she a twenty-nine-year-old married woman who wore the bonds of matrimony as loosely as he did. His reply (2 February 1929) to a letter in which she had asked him the second oldest question in the world ('Are you Thru with me?') implies that his final copulations took place during that encounter.

During these last years his house was kept for him
by the efficient Mrs Alice Laden, one of the nurses
who had attended the dying Charlotte. Mrs Laden
defended his privacy so doughtily against chance
callers, interlopers, scroungers, importuning journalists, autograph hunters and so forth, that she was
given the nickname St George's Dragon and gloried
in it to the extent of wearing a little dragon brooch
for a decoration.

As a Scotswoman and a trained nurse she would
have agreed that a steak washed down with a glass of
whisky would do an ageing vegetarian all the good in
the world. But although she had much influence with
him he was unshakeable on the steak question. She
did, however, surreptitiously add a little whisky to
his soup, with what effect on his health and behaviour
it would be difficult to gauge. To mention that after
dinner on a Sunday evening in September 1950, at
the age of ninety-four years and two months, he went
into the garden, climbed a tree and fell off it, might
suggest that the soup has been too well fortified.
But as a summary of the events of that fateful evening this is more Shavian than accurate.

That Sunday was the first day of one of the rare
holidays Mrs Laden ventured to take. She went off
to Aberdeen, leaving the house and its master in
charge of an Irishwoman, Mrs Ronald Smith (formerly
his highly regarded housemaid Margaret Cashin).
After dinner Shaw went into the garden and mounted
a ladder to prune a greengage tree. He had a haversack
on his back, presumably to receive the prunings, for
he was obsessively neat. The haversack may have
helped to overbalance him, and he fell off the ladder.
He invariably carried, when going out of doors, a
whistle on a cord around his neck. With this he
summoned help. Mrs Smith ran out and somehow
managed to get him back to the house and up to bed.

Being in great pain he assumed he had broken his back, but the doctor was able to reassure him on this point. [151]

The ambulance men who carried him downstairs on his way to hospital must have been surprised, as they laid him on the stretcher, to hear the aged patient exclaim, 'Thank God for that. If you'd dropped me then you'd have broken my bloody back.'

He was brought to Luton and Dunstable General Hospital where his leg was set and he was subjected to a kidney operation. He survived the ordeal and, according to the doctors, would have been a centenarian if only he had agreed to a second operation. But he was weary of life, he said, and asked to be let die without further interference. Somewhat inconsistently he complained that the nurses brought him only enough porridge to feed George but not Bernard. He lamented that other nurses were washing him away and were forcing him to drink when he did not wish to. Of one nurse he said to his doctor, 'The only way to get rid of that woman is to bury her.'

Before a BBC broadcast of *In Good King Charles's Golden Days* the leading lady, coming specially to the microphone to send a get well message, was mercifully spared the knowledge that she merely caused him to shoot up in his hospital bed and roar, 'Go to hell the lot of you.'

He insisted on being allowed home, and was accordingly brought back to Ayot, a shadow of a shadow. He lingered for a few weeks, two nurses in attendance. Courteous to the last, he received some relations and friends, always a trial to the gravely ill and a dreadful affliction to those whose only remaining desire is to be let drift quietly to their ending.

The last time he took a pen in his hand was to sign some income tax papers.

Mrs Laden watched over him to the end. When he

repeated to her that he wanted to die she said, 'I
wish it was I that was dying and not you.'

'You wouldn't if you'd had to go through what
I've had to.'

He lapsed into coma, a state in which, said Mrs
Laden, he kept snorting distressingly and looking
dreadful, although 'his heartbeat was magnificent
right up to the last. He had the heart of a lion.' It
ceased to beat at five in the morning of 2 November
1950.

'When he was dead,' she said, 'he looked wonderful — quite different.'

Index